LIVE INTO YOUR best life

52 WEEKS OF MICRO-WINS
TO TRANSFORM YOUR LIFE

CONTENT BY
PAULIE SKAJA

DESIGN BY
TAYLOR BELL

Live Into Your Best Life:
52 Weeks of Micro-Wins to Transform Your Life

ISBN: 979-8-9883115-2-2

Published by TH3 Publishing House
Paulie Skaja, LLC
PaulieSkaja.com

This book is dedicated to my children, Heather and Taylor; the inspiration that drives me to do my best and keep getting better each day.

INTRODUCTION

If you are reading these words, it's likely that you have decided something in your life needs to change. Perhaps you've noticed that your life feels empty. Maybe you are considering a career change so you can get off the proverbial hamster wheel. It's possible that you have noticed you've outgrown some of the people in your life. It may be that you have a wonderful life, and you want to simply make continuous improvements, so it keeps getting better.

These are all really great reasons to have picked up this book and it will help you as far as you are willing to take action and help yourself. With any DIY (do it yourself) approach, buying a book or taking a class does little to actually change your situation unless you act upon that internal desire.

This book is a guide to help you make incremental changes in any and/or all areas of your life. While there is logic to the order of the topics, you can work through the book in whatever order you feel compelled.

How many times have you made decisions based on what other people think or believe? Do you even realize when you're making choices that are derived from the beliefs of someone else? Let that go. As you work through this book, you are in complete control of your approach and your outcomes. In fact, no one can do the work for you. It's all done by you and for you. It's all you!

Imagine how your life could change if you started to pay attention to what you're thinking and believing with the intent of choosing what's best for you and the life you want to create for yourself. Do you know how you would like your life to be? You may know you want something to change, but are you clear on what isn't working for you and how you'd like things to be different?

If you do, that's great! If you don't, that's just fine!

Right now, that's all you need to do. Get really clear on what part of your life you'd like to change or improve. If you're using this book to lift your life to the next level, then that's your goal. If you want to use it to focus on a specific area of your life, now is the time to bring that awareness to the forefront and figure out how you want things to be for you instead.

When you know that you are unhappy with an area of your life, but you lack clarity on how you would like things to be, it's like setting out on a vacation and saying you want to "go west." With no clear idea of where you want to end up, you could go in that direction for five miles and return home and you would have still gone west yet that is probably not your idea of a vacation nor was that likely your intended destination.

While I love to go with the flow and allow opportunities to emerge, I've learned that if I'm really unhappy with an aspect of my life, but I have no idea how I'd like things to be different, nothing will change. I can only make changes in my actions, my beliefs, and my choices. I cannot change anyone else.

That's why it is so important for you to consider what part of your life you want to be different and how you want it to be.

Let's say you want a different dynamic with a person in your life. If you're hoping the other person will change how they're acting or behaving to make you happy, then you will likely be disappointed. While you can explain to them how their behavior impacts you and hope they choose to listen and change their ways because they want to be in a harmonious relationship with you, chances are their behavior will revert to their normal state after some time because they are actually fine with the dynamic.

If you truly cannot tolerate the interaction any longer, then you have a decision to make. How would you like things to be? What do you need to change to create that outcome?

You may want to change how you spend time together so there are fewer opportunities for these behaviors to trigger you. You may want to just breathe through the circumstances and let them go knowing that this is how things are. You may choose to remove this person from your life. You have options. You cannot change someone else; you can only change yourself.

This is true for any area of your life. Simply replace the focus of the relationship in the previous scenario with your career, your well-being, your financial health, and so on. You are in control of your life.

Now, take some time to get clear on what needs to change in your life and how you would like things to be instead. When you're clear on what you want and how you want things to be, you will engage your Reticular Activating System (RAS). Your RAS helps you see what you are looking for more easily.

> Note: If you focus on what you don't want, you will bring more of it into your life because you will see and attract what you are focused on. With that in mind, if you know what you don't want, then consider what you do want. How you want things to be may not be the opposite of what you don't want, so be really clear on what you want and how you want things to be.

The concepts in this book are based on Neuro-Linguistic Programming (NLP). NLP asserts that there is a connection between neurological processes, language and your behavioral patterns, and that these can be changed to achieve specific goals in your life. The words you read, think, and say impact how you live your life and by changing your thoughts and beliefs you can change your life.

Once you're clear on your intention, you will make this your focus...at least for the week. If your focus changes or a new topic emerges, just go with it. This is your RAS, your internal guidance system, bringing the most relevant opportunities to light so you can start to live into your best life.

HOW TO USE THIS BOOK

Are you ready to start this journey? Are you ready to take action? Are you ready to live into your best life? Even if you didn't respond with a resounding, "YES," every journey starts with the first step.

Your first step is to decide if you're going to work this book from front to back like following step-by-step instructions, or if you're going to be more adventurous and open the book to a new spot each week, trusting that the message on that page is perfect for where you are in the moment.

Another decision you get to make is when you want to capture your thoughts for the day. Some people choose to make their notes just before going to bed at night, while others choose a specific time each day. It doesn't matter when you make your notes as long as you make them daily. You may be thinking, "But what if life gets in the way?" or "What if I forget?" That's ok, just make your notes as soon as you're able.

> Insider's tip: Consistency is how people make progress and achieve what others believe is impossible. Set your intention and take action. It's that simple. It's not easy, but it is simple. If you miss a day, just think back and write about what comes up for you.

Now that you know which approach you are going to use to work through the book and you know when you are going to record your insights, it's time to get started.

Read the thought at the top of the page for the week you've chosen. Take a moment to consider what this message means to you and notice what emotions or feelings it evokes. Now, go about your day. At the time you have chosen, make notes regarding what came up for you around this topic and how it applies to the day's activities. While you may question how this random idea or quote can help you transform your life, I encourage you to let go of logic and just trust me. You have nothing to lose and infinite possibilities to gain.

By the way, as you record the thoughts that come up for you, you may also want to capture your daily micro-wins. These are accomplishments that you've made throughout the day. They can be something small, like you made time to take a walk. They can be something significant, such as finding the courage to speak up in a meeting or having a difficult conversation with someone even though that person may get upset. Whatever it is, these actions are taken by you, for you, to support your journey.

At the end of the week, take a few extra moments to reflect. Did you make choices and decisions based on what you want, or did you consider what you believe others would have you decide or choose? Did you shift your outcome once you had this awareness, or did you realize your response aligns with what you really want as well? What other ah-hah moments did you discover? Capture them and notice how they make you feel.

Last, determine how you want to celebrate your progress. I'm all about finding ways to celebrate even what seem to be small wins. I find this helps motivate me to continue taking action and making progress. Perhaps it will work for you too.

Are you ready to take action so you can live into your best life?

- Have you set your intention?
- Are you going to follow the journey from front to back or create your own adventure?
- Do you know what time each day you will capture your thoughts from that day's activities?

Let's Do This!

WEEK ONE

"Everybody puts their pants on one leg at a time"
~ Cliff Skaja
monday
tuesday
wednesday

We are all people doing the best we can each day. When did you notice yourself being authentic in the presence of others regardless of their position or status? What micro-wins did you experience? Capture your thoughts, actions and decisions daily.

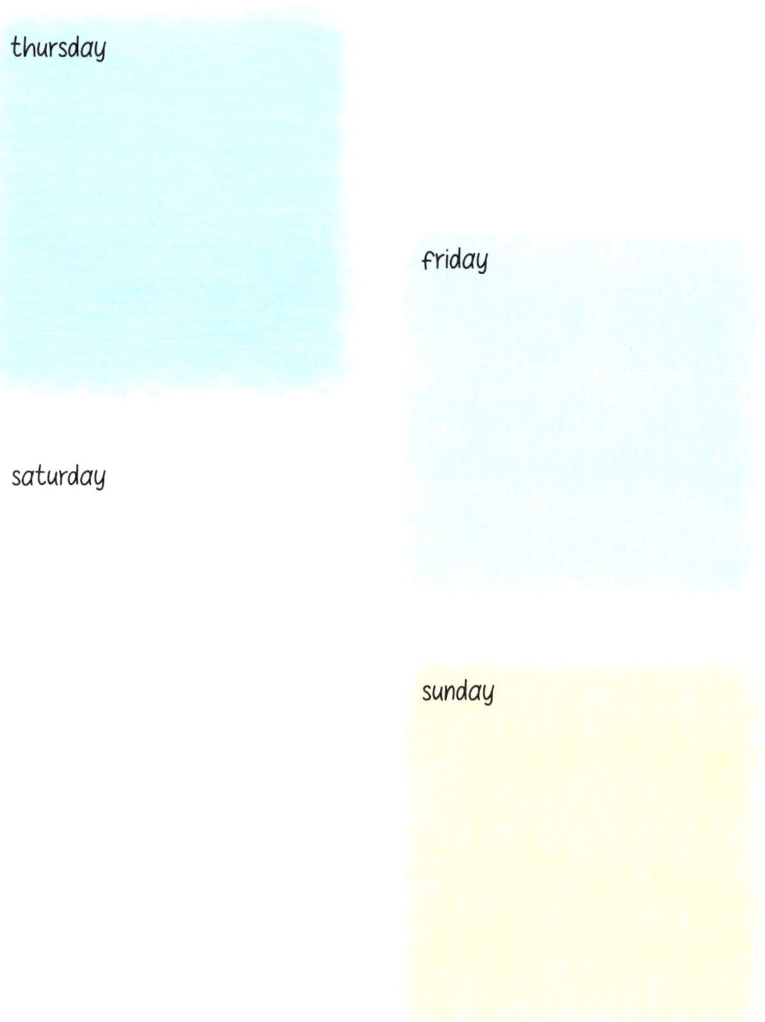

What have you learned about yourself that you can carry forward into the weeks, months, and years to come? What are you ready to let go of so you can live into your best life? Small actions each week will lead to big results.

Well done!

What have you learned about yourself this week? What micro-wins will you celebrate this week? How does it make you feel to acknowledge these achievements?

WEEK TWO

Remember to BREATHE.

Inhale. Exhale. Inhale. Exhale. Inhale. Exhale. Inhale. Exhale.

Most of us hold our breath throughout the day without realizing. Remembering to breathe is also a great way to break state. If something makes you feel upset or triggers a response you would rather avoid, taking a few moments to purposefully breathe will help that feeling pass and allow you to move forward with intent. How has remembering to breathe supported your journey? What micro-wins did you experience? Capture your thoughts, actions and decisions daily.

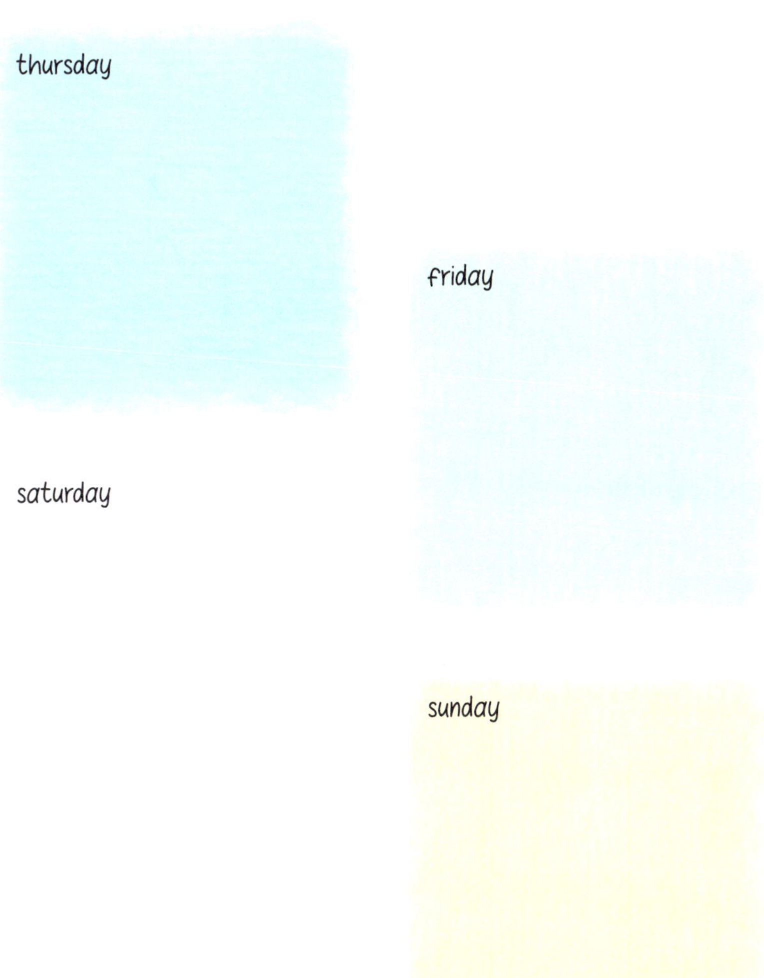

What have you learned about yourself that you can carry forward into the weeks, months, and years to come? What are you ready to let go of so you can live into your best life? Small actions each week will lead to big results.

Well done!

What have you learned about yourself this week? What micro-wins will you celebrate this week? How does it make you feel to acknowledge these achievements?

WEEK THREE

Each moment is a new beginning.

We all have 24 hours, 1,440 minutes, and 86,400 seconds in each day to make new choices and start fresh.

When you notice that you have made a choice or decision that is out of alignment with how you want things to be, you can take that moment to make a new choice or decision and get back on track. When did you pause and pivot? How did it make you feel to realize you didn't fail, but instead, you were actually successful? What micro-wins did you experience? Capture your thoughts, actions and decisions daily.

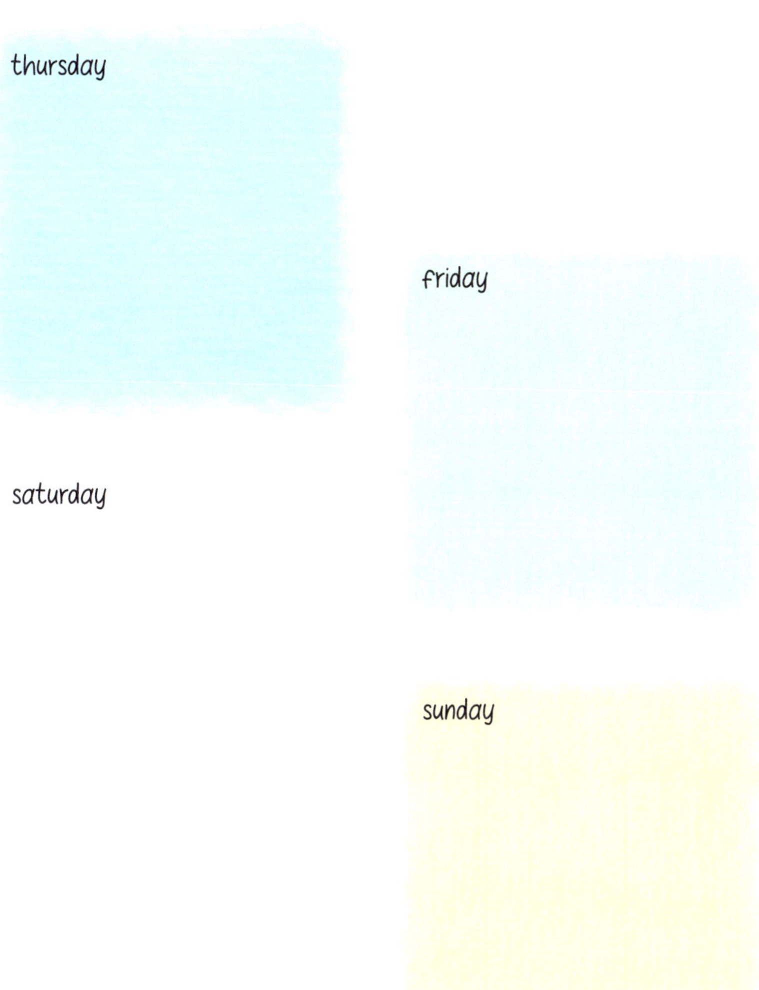

What have you learned about yourself that you can carry forward into the weeks, months, and years to come? What are you ready to let go of so you can live into your best life? Small actions each week will lead to big results.

Well done!

What have you learned about yourself this week? What micro-wins will you celebrate this week? How does it make you feel to acknowledge these achievements?

WEEK FOUR

Learn something new each day.

Perhaps it's a new word, or how to do something you have always wanted to try. Keep expanding your knowledge.

Perhaps you learned something about yourself or someone else. Maybe you chose to research something you have been curious about. By expanding your knowledge each day, you become more open to new possibilities. What did you learn today? What micro-wins did you experience? Capture your thoughts, actions and decisions daily.

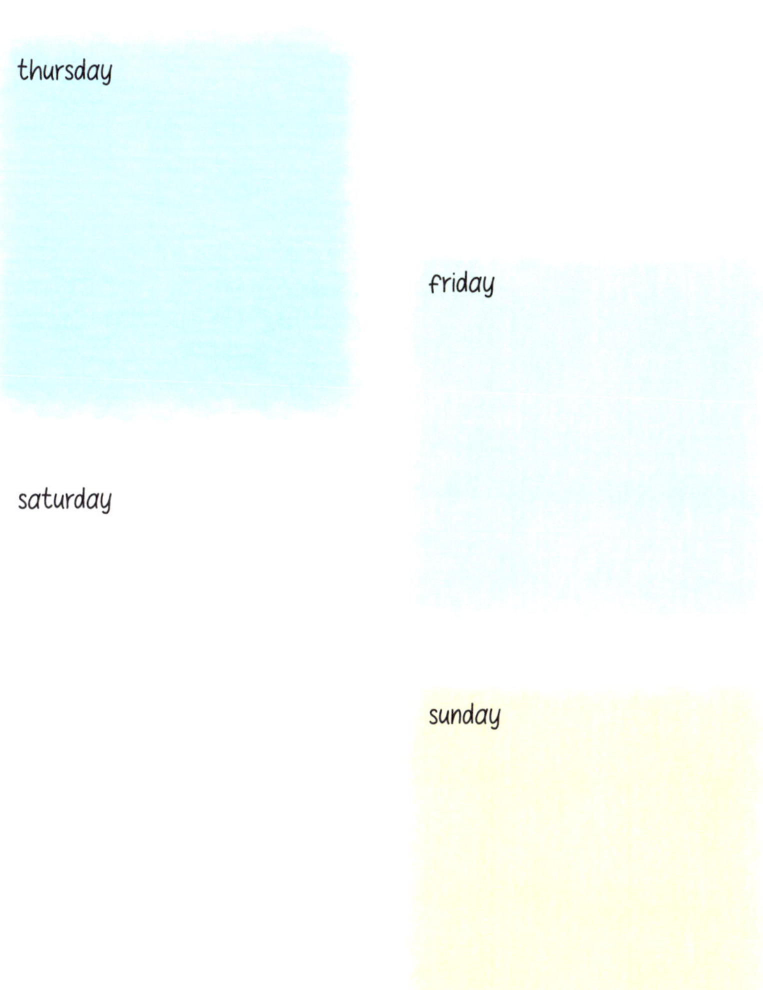

What have you learned about yourself that you can carry forward into the weeks, months, and years to come? What are you ready to let go of so you can live into your best life? Small actions each week will lead to big results.

Well done!

What have you learned about yourself this week? What micro-wins will you celebrate this week? How does it make you feel to acknowledge these achievements?

WEEK FIVE

Try something new each day.

By trying new things, you create new connections and fire off more neurons in your brain, creating plasticity.

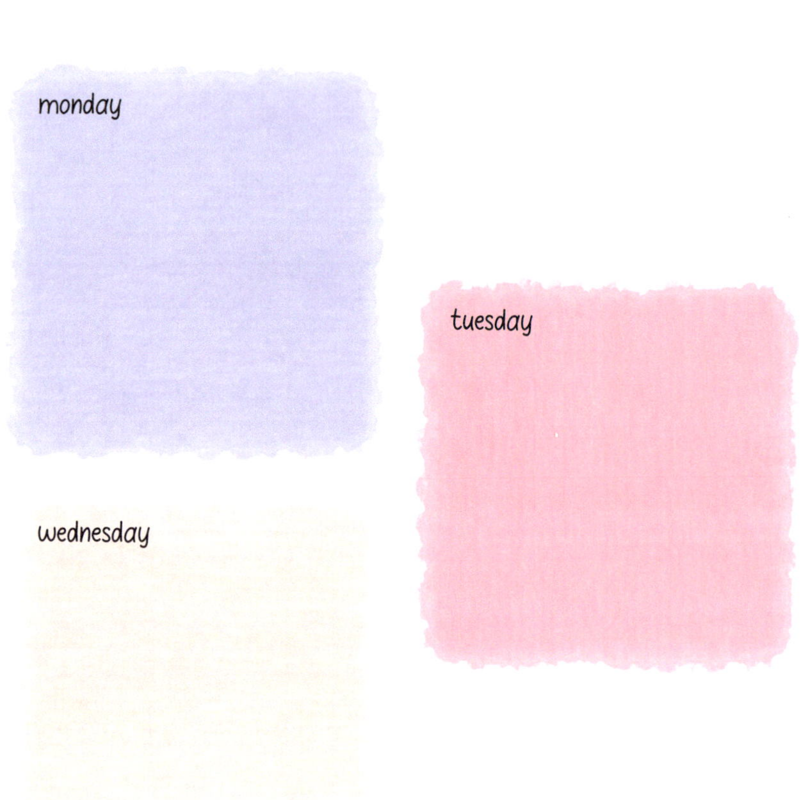

When you try something new, you are building new neural pathways and enhancing existing ones to help keep your brain active and healthy. What new things did you try each day? Did you enjoy it or realize you don't need to do that again? What micro-wins did you experience? Capture your thoughts, actions and decisions daily.

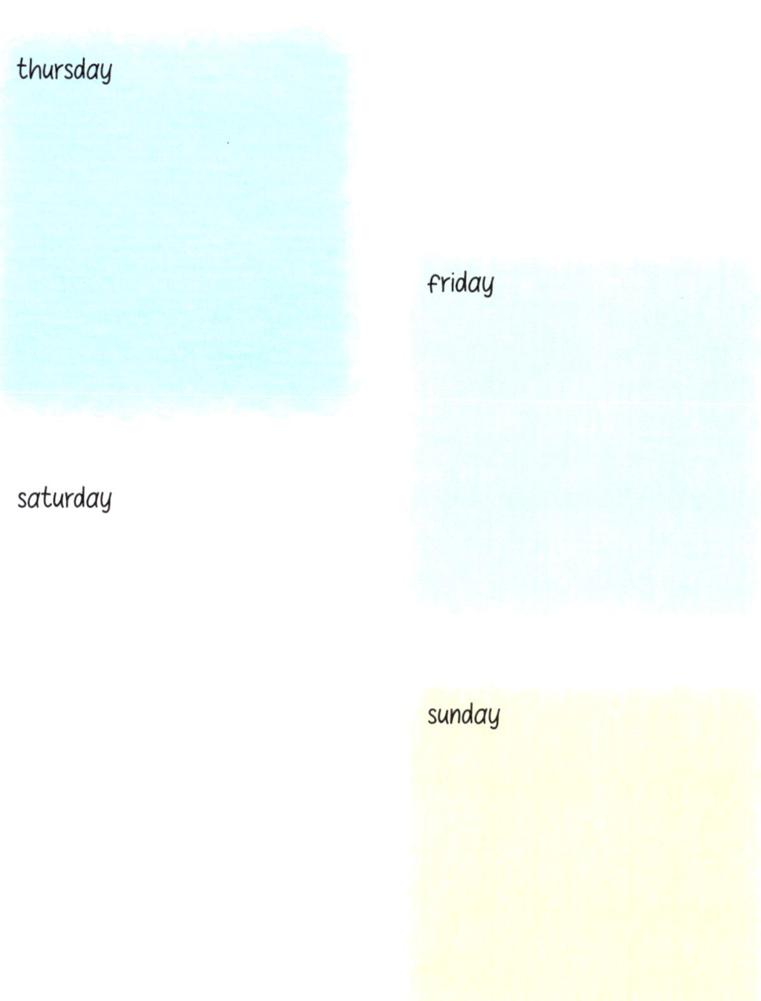

What have you learned about yourself that you can carry forward into the weeks, months, and years to come? What are you ready to let go of so you can live into your best life? Small actions each week will lead to big results.

Well done!

What have you learned about yourself this week? What micro-wins will you celebrate this week? How does it make you feel to acknowledge these achievements?

WEEK SIX

Remember to make time to play.

Although people think playing is for children, it actually helps us be more creative while making our day more fun.

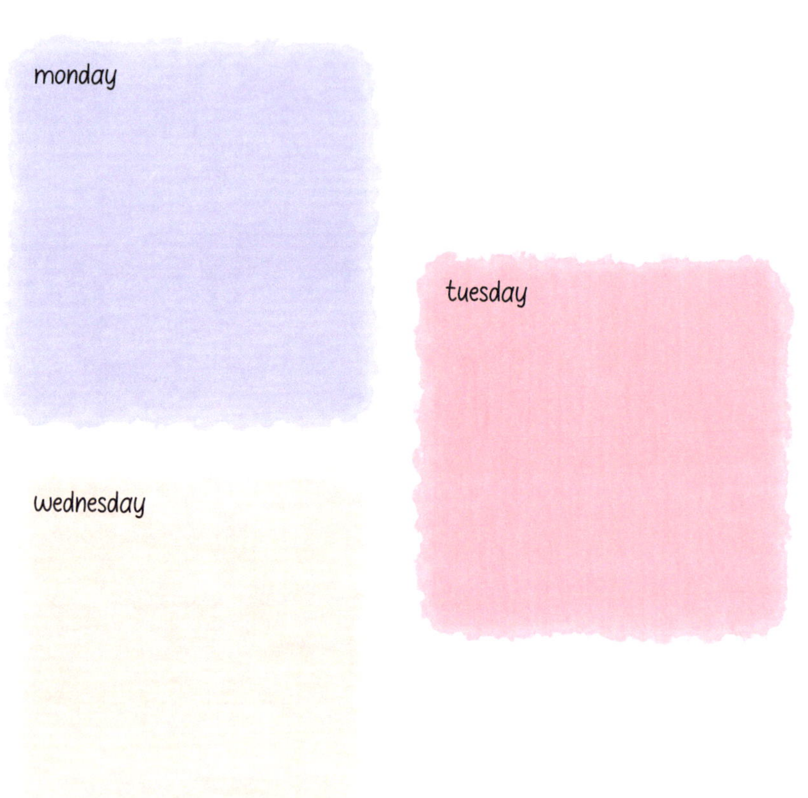

As adults, we tend to take life too seriously. At some point in your past, someone may have told you to "act your age" or "stop fooling around." By restricting your thoughts and actions, you are also restricting your ability to be creative, to think outside the box and to come up with new solutions to problems. How have you played today? What micro-wins did you experience? Capture your thoughts, actions and decisions daily.

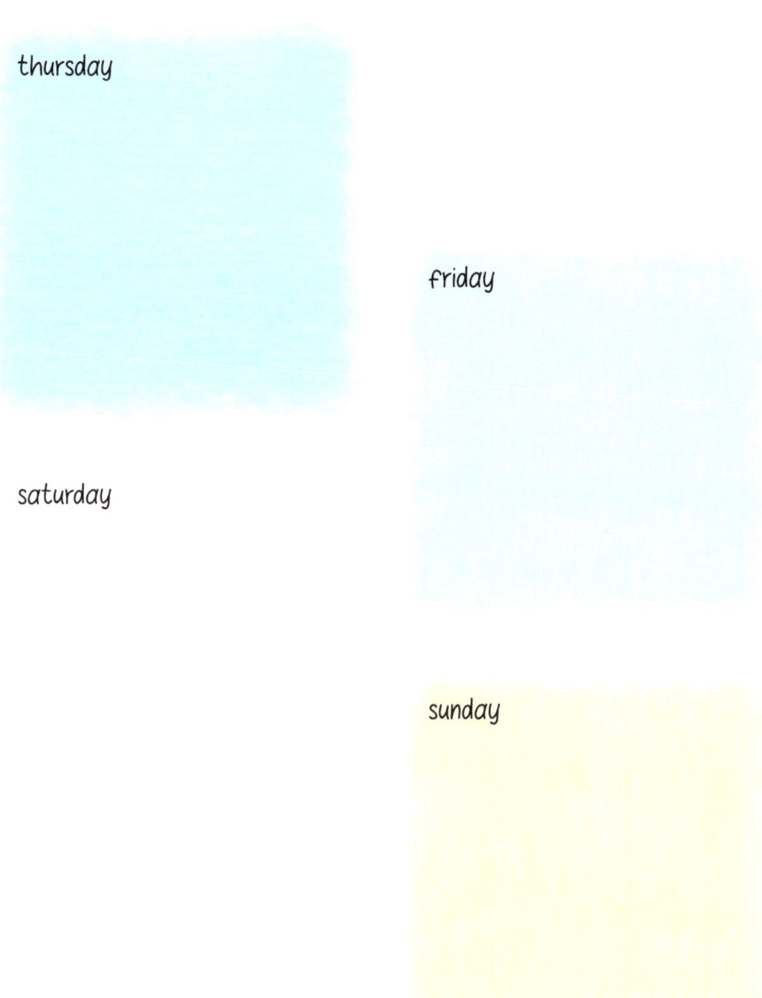

What have you learned about yourself that you can carry forward into the weeks, months, and years to come? What are you ready to let go of so you can live into your best life? Small actions each week will lead to big results.

Well done!

What have you learned about yourself this week? What micro-wins will you celebrate this week? How does it make you feel to acknowledge these achievements?

WEEK SEVEN

"Life is short. Live each moment to the fullest."

– Cliff Skaja

monday

tuesday

wednesday

We never know when we will take our last breath. If you knew today was your last day on Earth, what would you do differently? As you go through each day, notice if you are doing what you really want to be doing and if not, what can you change to live your life more fully? What micro-wins did you experience? Capture your thoughts, actions and decisions daily.

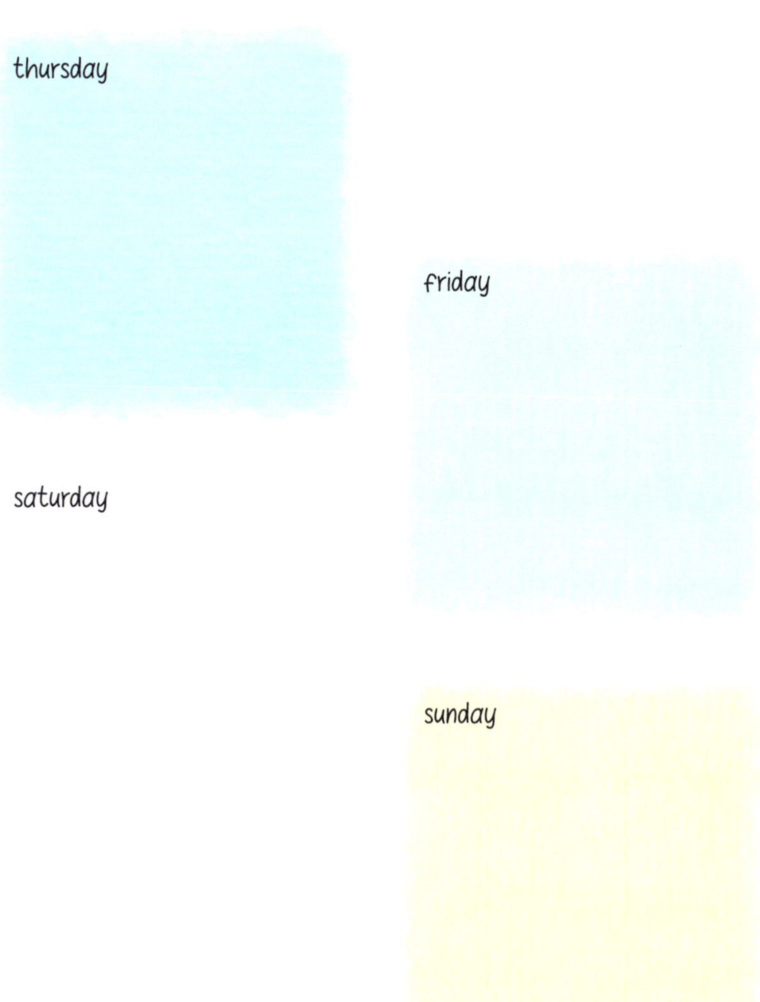

What have you learned about yourself that you can carry forward into the weeks, months, and years to come? What are you ready to let go of so you can live into your best life? Small actions each week will lead to big results.

Well done!

What have you learned about yourself this week? What micro-wins will you celebrate this week? How does it make you feel to acknowledge these achievements?

WEEK EIGHT

Find 3 things to be grateful for each day.

Gratitude is a way of acknowledging the good things in life and supports a positive cognitive mind set.

You may have heard the saying, "What we focus on is what we get." When you focus on the things you are thankful for you will begin to notice more opportunities for gratitude. What are you grateful for today? What micro-wins did you experience? Capture your thoughts, actions and decisions daily.

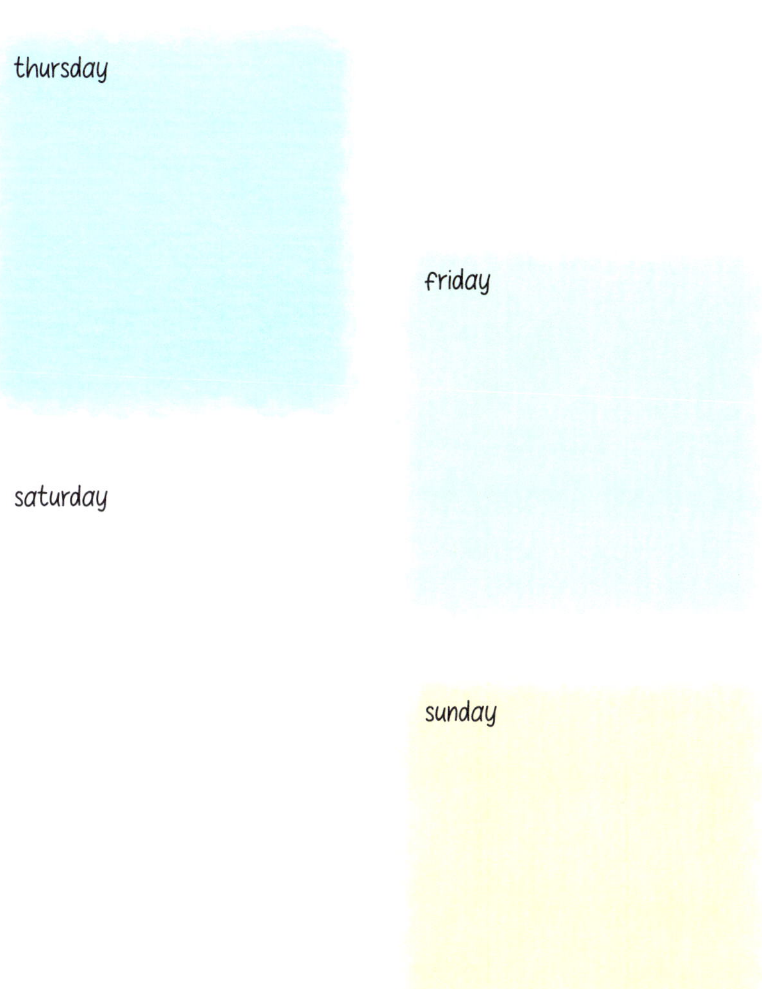

What have you learned about yourself that you can carry forward into the weeks, months, and years to come? What are you ready to let go of so you can live into your best life? Small actions each week will lead to big results.

Well done!

What have you learned about yourself this week? What micro-wins will you celebrate this week? How does it make you feel to acknowledge these achievements?

WEEK NINE

Life is a journey.

Enjoy the experiences along the way and take time to smell the roses (or coffee).

monday

tuesday

wednesday

Although you may want to snap your fingers and have your life be exactly how you think you want it, by going on this journey, you get to discover new experiences that may take you down new paths. What did you discover on your journey today? What micro-wins did you experience? Capture your thoughts, actions and decisions daily.

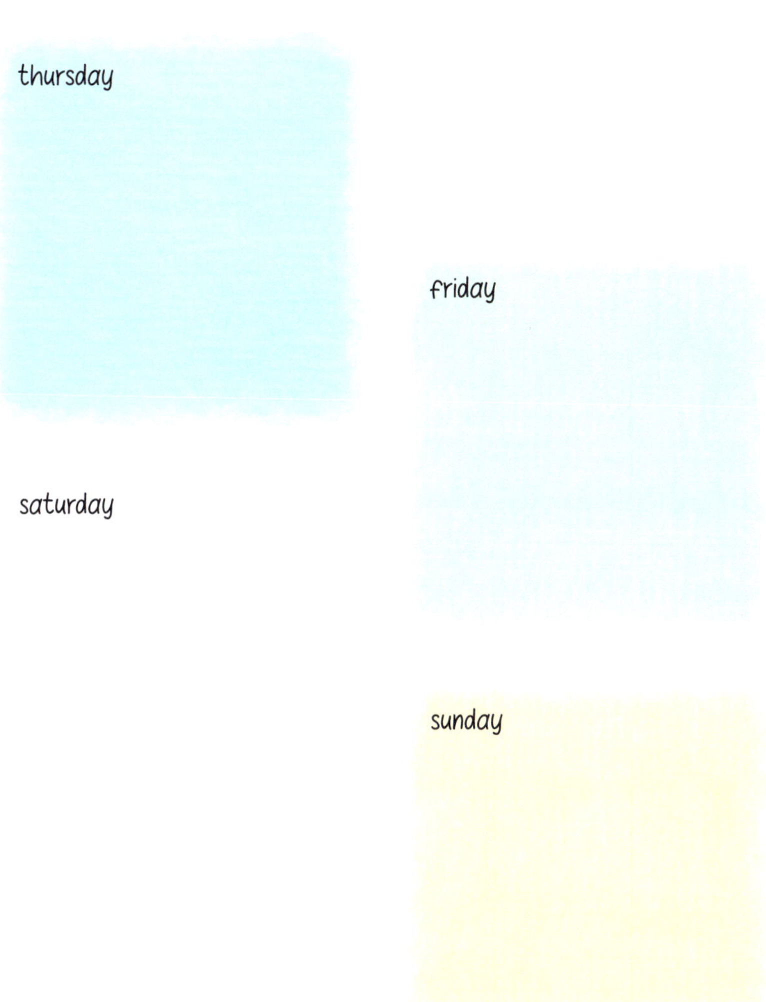

What have you learned about yourself that you can carry forward into the weeks, months, and years to come? What are you ready to let go of so you can live into your best life? Small actions each week will lead to big results.

Well done!

What have you learned about yourself this week? What micro-wins will you celebrate this week? How does it make you feel to acknowledge these achievements?

WEEK TEN

Mistakes / failures are steppingstones.

When things don't go as planned, learn from the outcomes, determine how to improve, and continue on.

monday

tuesday

wednesday

Life is an iterative journey filled with trial and error. If you do everything perfectly all the time, you may cease to learn or grow. In fact, you are probably playing small. What didn't go perfectly today? What did you learn and what can you do differently next time to improve? What micro-wins did you experience? Capture your thoughts, actions and decisions daily.

thursday

friday

saturday

sunday

What have you learned about yourself that you can carry forward into the weeks, months, and years to come? What are you ready to let go of so you can live into your best life? Small actions each week will lead to big results.

Well done!

What have you learned about yourself this week? What micro-wins will you celebrate this week? How does it make you feel to acknowledge these achievements?

WEEK ELEVEN

Overwhelm tends to be an indication of lack of clarity.

If you are feeling confused or overwhelmed, it often means you need more information to proceed.

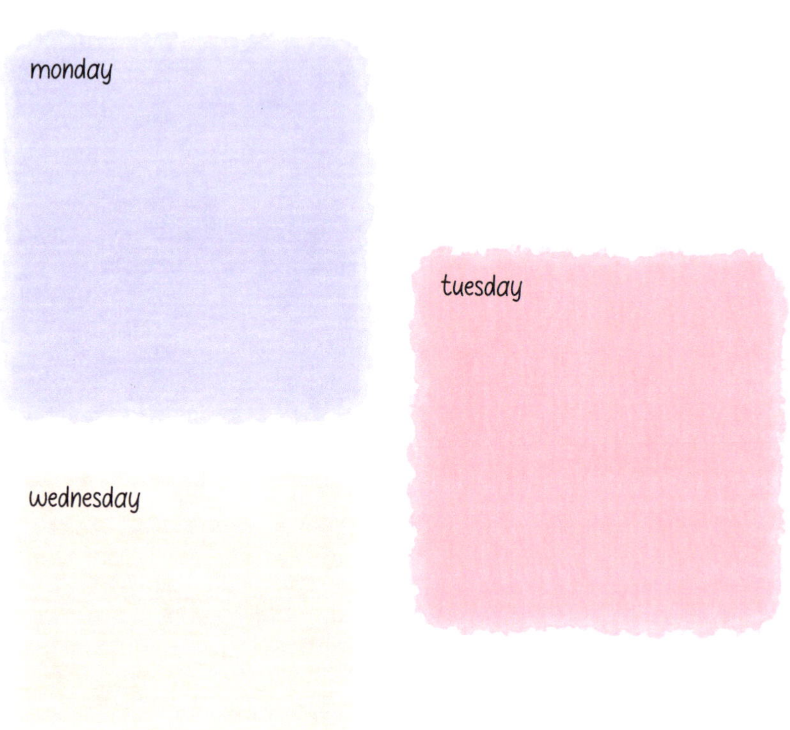

When life is moving too fast or you feel like things are coming at you from all directions or you're struggling to make decisions, these are often indications that you are trying to take action without all the information you need to be successful. Where do you need more clarity? What micro-wins did you experience? Capture your thoughts, actions and decisions daily.

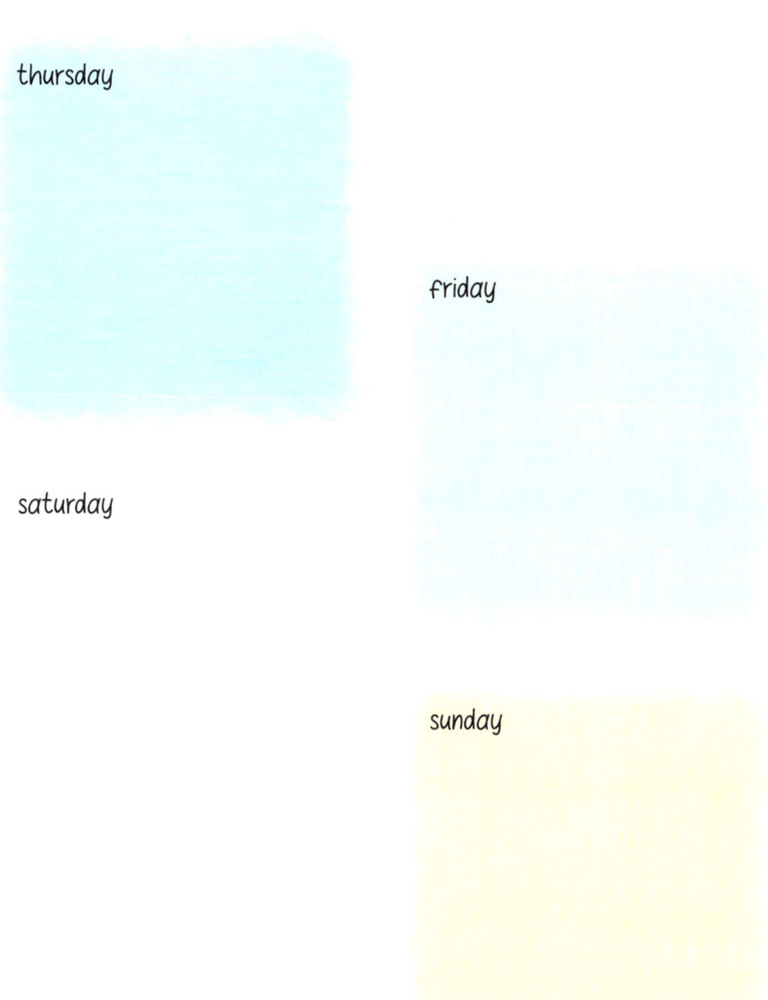

What have you learned about yourself that you can carry forward into the weeks, months, and years to come? What are you ready to let go of so you can live into your best life? Small actions each week will lead to big results.

Well done!

What have you learned about yourself this week? What micro-wins will you celebrate this week? How does it make you feel to acknowledge these achievements?

WEEK TWELVE

Always do your best.

Each day, your best will be different based on how that day is going in those circumstances and that is perfect.

monday

tuesday

wednesday

Taken from the book, *The Four Agreements*, the fourth agreement is to always do your best. Your best will change from day to day. Avoid judging yourself or comparing yourself to others. How did you do your best today? What micro-wins did you experience? Capture your thoughts, actions and decisions daily.

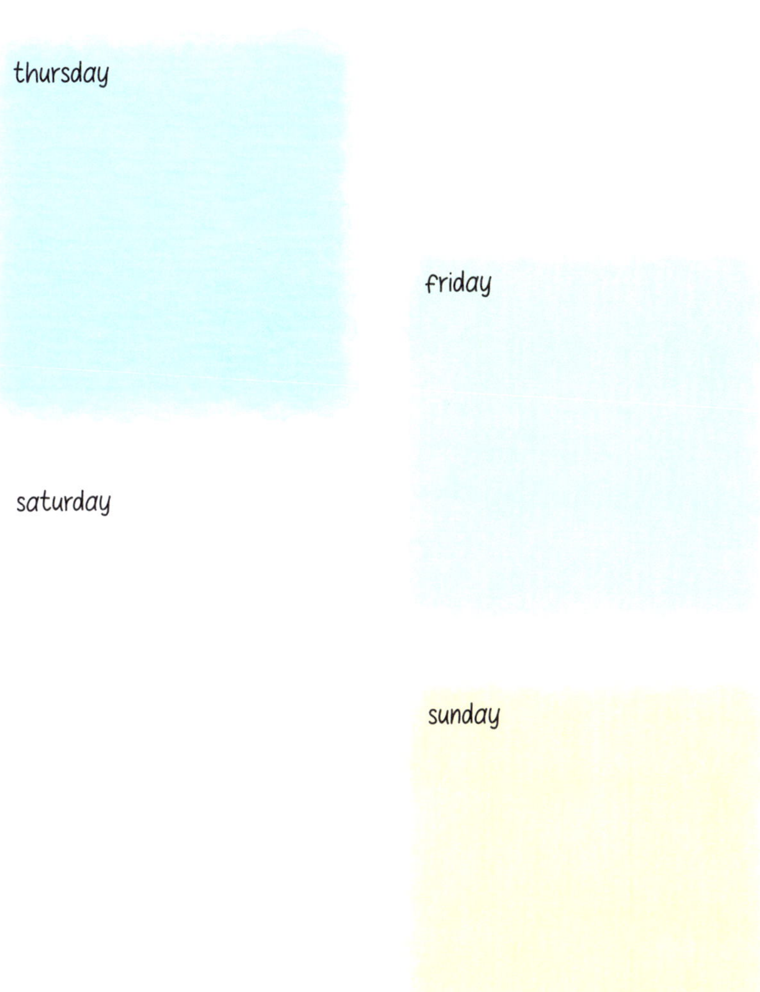

What have you learned about yourself that you can carry forward into the weeks, months, and years to come? What are you ready to let go of so you can live into your best life? Small actions each week will lead to big results.

Well done!

What have you learned about yourself this week? What micro-wins will you celebrate this week? How does it make you feel to acknowledge these achievements?

WEEK THIRTEEN

"You can do, be and have anything you want as long as you really want it."

~ Cliff Skaja

monday

tuesday

wednesday

You can create the life you want. The key is that you really need to want it for yourself. If you are living life to make others happy, you will miss each time. What do you really want and how did you take action towards these desires? What micro-wins did you experience? Capture your thoughts, actions and decisions daily.

thursday

friday

saturday

sunday

What have you learned about yourself that you can carry forward into the weeks, months, and years to come? What are you ready to let go of so you can live into your best life? Small actions each week will lead to big results.

Well done!

What have you learned about yourself this week? What micro-wins will you celebrate this week? How does it make you feel to acknowledge these achievements?

WEEK FOURTEEN

Follow the breadcrumbs and notice the signs.

Our internal guidance system shows us clues to help us achieve our goals if we just pay attention.

monday

tuesday

wednesday

The RAS (reticular activating system) is your internal guidance system that shows you clues to help you achieve your goals if you just pay attention. What signs did you notice that can help you achieve success? What micro-wins did you experience? Capture your thoughts, actions and decisions daily.

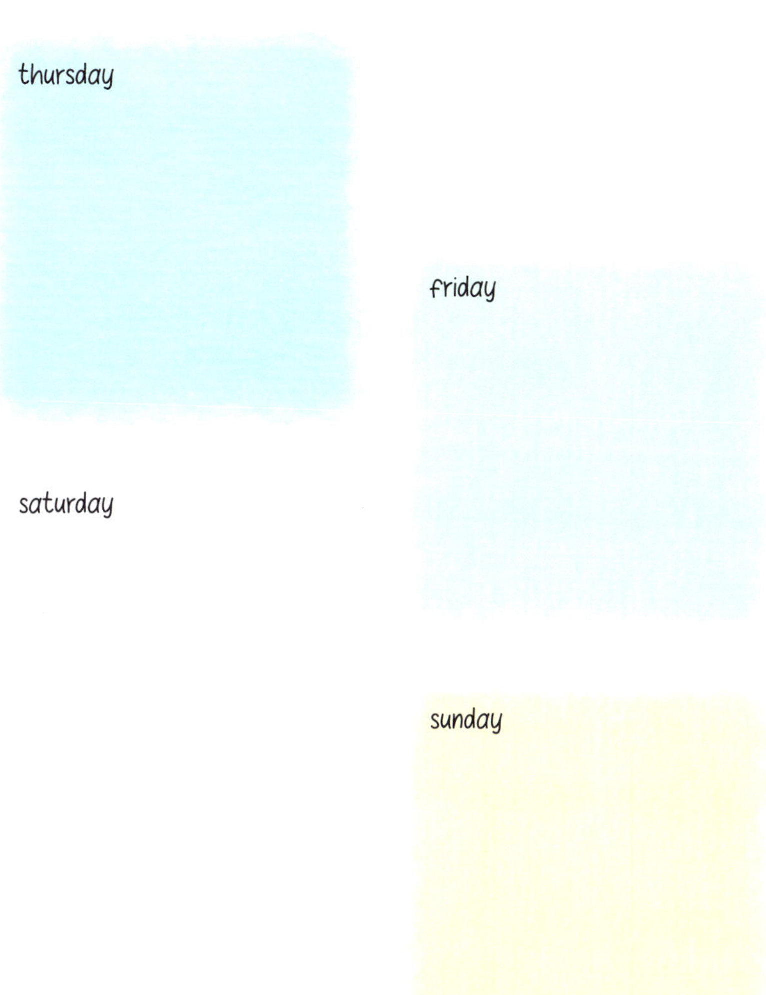

What have you learned about yourself that you can carry forward into the weeks, months, and years to come? What are you ready to let go of so you can live into your best life? Small actions each week will lead to big results.

Well done!

What have you learned about yourself this week? What micro-wins will you celebrate this week? How does it make you feel to acknowledge these achievements?

WEEK FIFTEEN

Do what makes you happy.

Spend your time doing the things that fill your spirit with joy and make you happy.

monday

tuesday

wednesday

If you are living life to make others happy, do these choices make you happy too? If they do, then own it. No one can make you happy any more than you can make anyone else happy. What are you choosing that brings you happiness? What micro-wins did you experience? Capture your thoughts, actions and decisions daily.

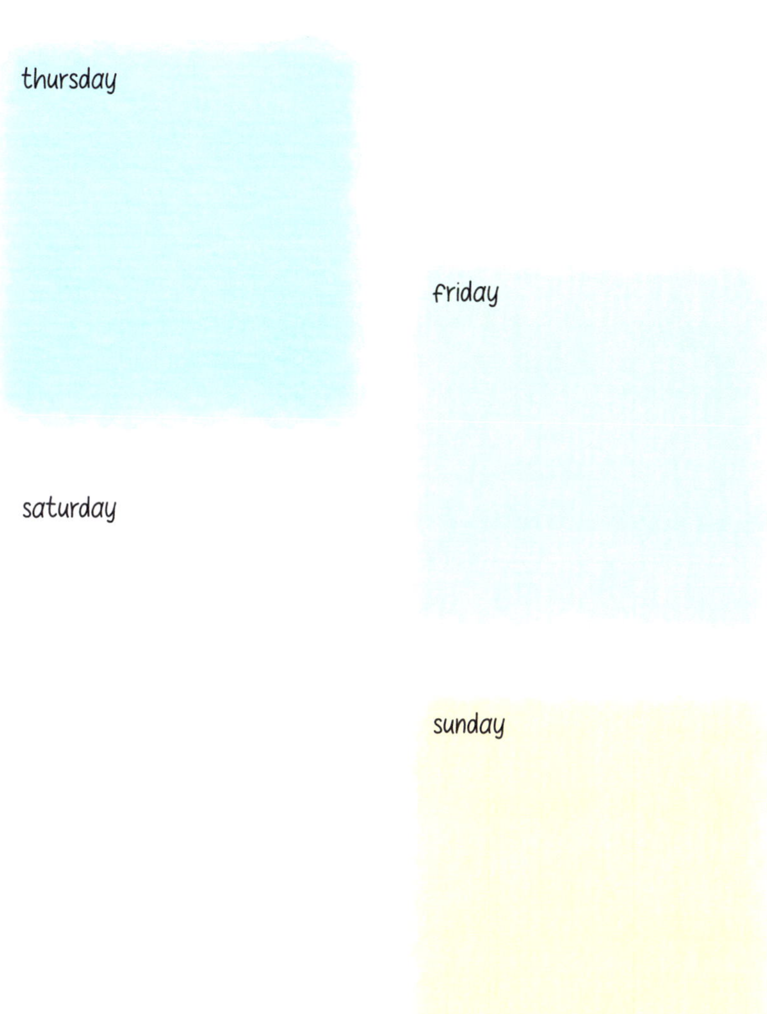

What have you learned about yourself that you can carry forward into the weeks, months, and years to come? What are you ready to let go of so you can live into your best life? Small actions each week will lead to big results.

Well done!

What have you learned about yourself this week? What micro-wins will you celebrate this week? How does it make you feel to acknowledge these achievements?

WEEK SIXTEEN

“What we resists persists.”

~ Carl Jung

When you strive to avoid something, you may notice that it keeps presenting itself so it can be addressed. Your RAS is providing an opportunity for growth and healing. What are you resisting that you get to deal with? What micro-wins did you experience? Capture your thoughts, actions and decisions daily.

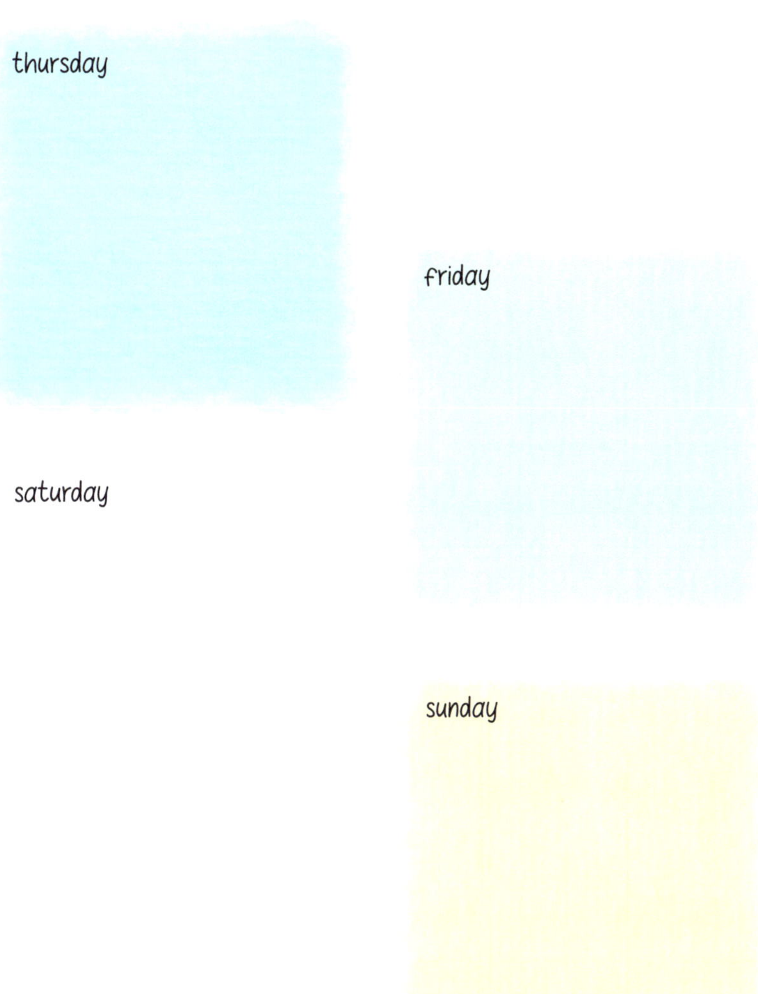

What have you learned about yourself that you can carry forward into the weeks, months, and years to come? What are you ready to let go of so you can live into your best life? Small actions each week will lead to big results.

Well done!

What have you learned about yourself this week? What micro-wins will you celebrate this week? How does it make you feel to acknowledge these achievements?

WEEK SEVENTEEN

"Move towards what you want rather than running away from what you don't want."

~ Paulie Skaja

monday

tuesday

wednesday

One truth is that where you go, there you are. If you find yourself wanting out of a situation, it's important that you get clear on how you would like things to be instead, otherwise you will find yourself in a new situation with the same circumstances. What would you like to move towards? What micro-wins did you experience? Capture your thoughts, actions and decisions daily.

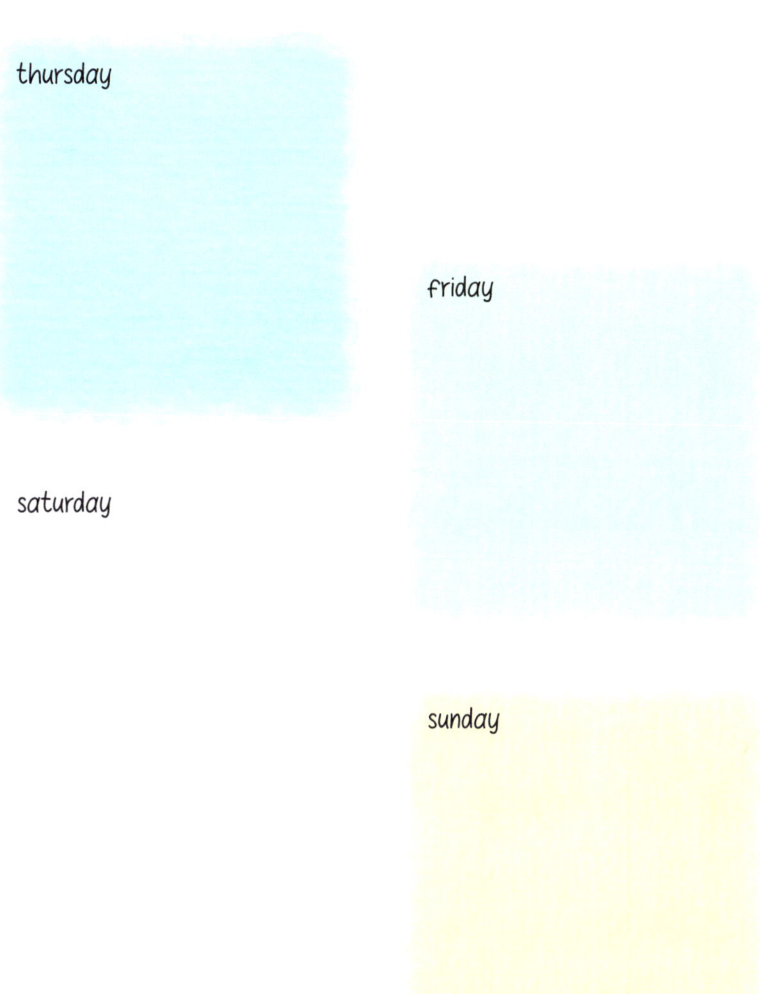

What have you learned about yourself that you can carry forward into the weeks, months, and years to come? What are you ready to let go of so you can live into your best life? Small actions each week will lead to big results.

Well done!

What have you learned about yourself this week? What micro-wins will you celebrate this week? How does it make you feel to acknowledge these achievements?

WEEK EIGHTEEN

Be yourself.

When you live as your authentic self, you are aligned with who you are meant to be.

monday

tuesday

wednesday

As a human being, you want to fit in. In order to do this, you learned at a young age to model the behaviors of the people around you. This survival technique caused you to conform rather than allow your natural style to emerge. How are you being more authentic each day? What micro-wins did you experience? Capture your thoughts, actions and decisions daily.

thursday

friday

saturday

sunday

What have you learned about yourself that you can carry forward into the weeks, months, and years to come? What are you ready to let go of so you can live into your best life? Small actions each week will lead to big results.

Well done!

What have you learned about yourself this week? What micro-wins will you celebrate this week? How does it make you feel to acknowledge these achievements?

WEEK NINETEEN

"Never ask someone to do what you aren't willing to do yourself."

~ Cliff Skaja

monday

tuesday

wednesday

This is a "rule" my dad, Cliff, lived by. There are things we would rather not do, but consider how it makes you feel when someone else asks you to do what they don't want to do. What are some things you can do rather than ask others? How did it make you feel? What micro-wins did you experience? Capture your thoughts, actions and decisions daily.

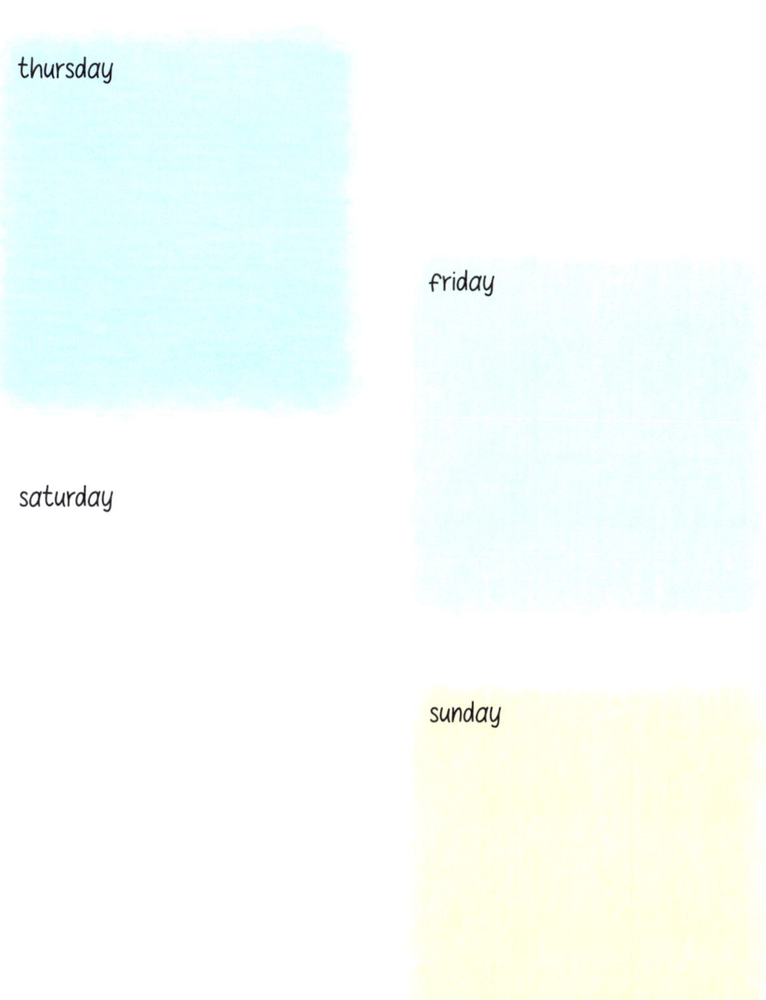

What have you learned about yourself that you can carry forward into the weeks, months, and years to come? What are you ready to let go of so you can live into your best life? Small actions each week will lead to big results.

Well done!

What have you learned about yourself this week? What micro-wins will you celebrate this week? How does it make you feel to acknowledge these achievements?

WEEK TWENTY

Never judge a book by its cover.

When you make assumptions based on how something or someone looks, you may miss out on so much more.

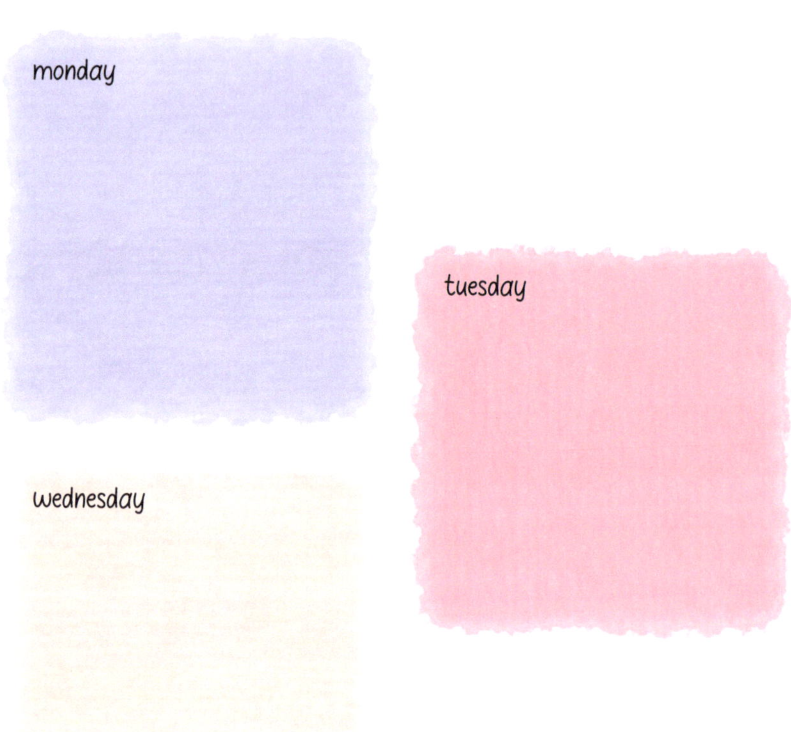

This concept dates back to the early 1700s and conveys the idea that most people strive to show only aspects of themselves and situations that are appealing for fear of being outcast. What judgements may you want to reconsider? What micro-wins did you experience? Capture your thoughts, actions and decisions daily.

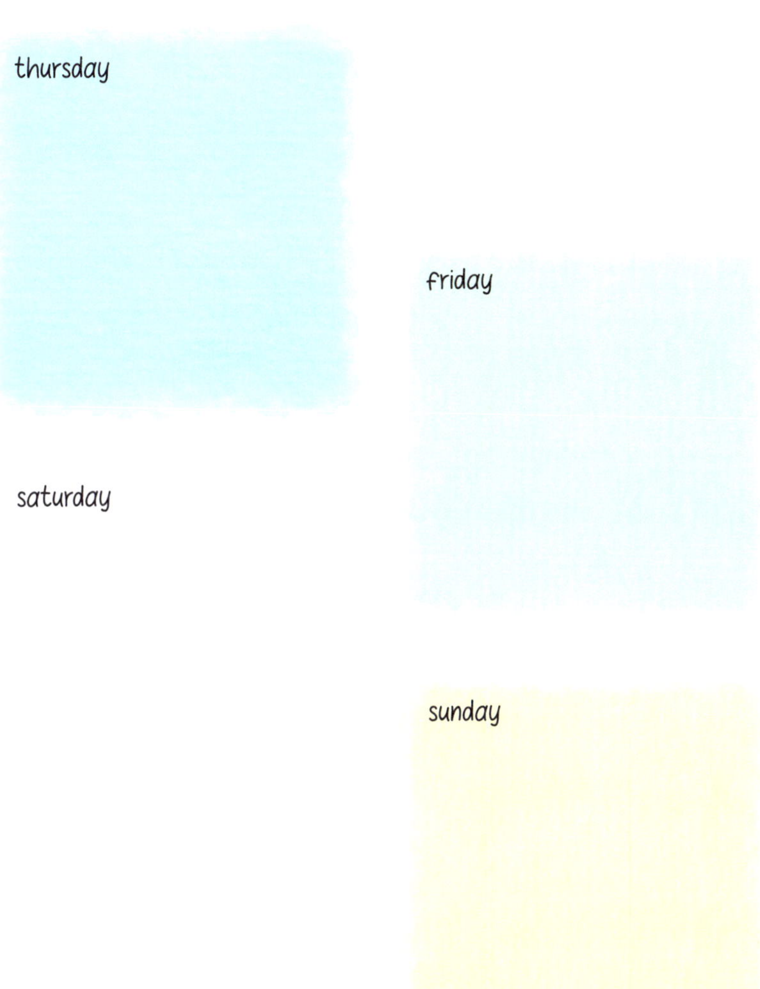

What have you learned about yourself that you can carry forward into the weeks, months, and years to come? What are you ready to let go of so you can live into your best life? Small actions each week will lead to big results.

Well done!

What have you learned about yourself this week? What micro-wins will you celebrate this week? How does it make you feel to acknowledge these achievements?

WEEK TWENTY-ONE

Surround yourself with people and things you enjoy.

Become aware of how the people and things you have in your life make you feel and adjust accordingly.

monday

tuesday

wednesday

Often, we fill our lives with people, experiences and things just to make our lives feel fuller. When is the last time you took an inventory of how the people, experiences and things in your life make you feel? What no longer brings you joy and how can you change that? What micro-wins did you experience? Capture your thoughts, actions and decisions daily.

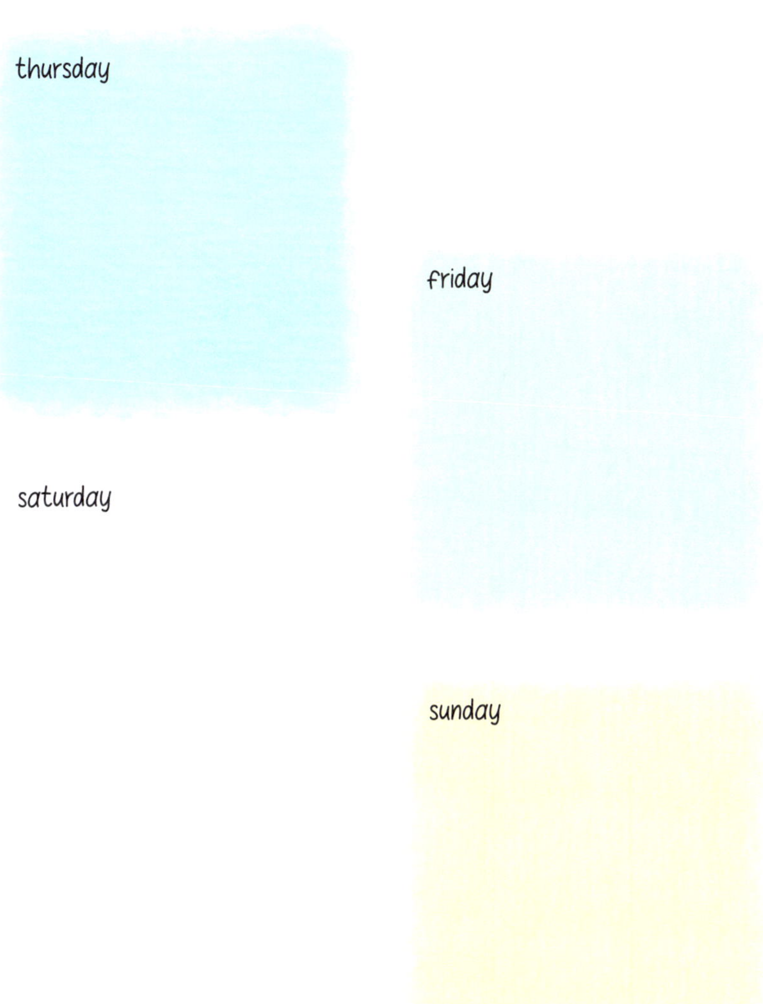

What have you learned about yourself that you can carry forward into the weeks, months, and years to come? What are you ready to let go of so you can live into your best life? Small actions each week will lead to big results.

Well done!

What have you learned about yourself this week? What micro-wins will you celebrate this week? How does it make you feel to acknowledge these achievements?

WEEK TWENTY-TWO

Forgive others for yourself, they don't care.

Forgiveness is about letting go of anger, resentment, and pain to set yourself free of the burden they carry.

monday

tuesday

wednesday

When you carry the baggage of heavy emotions, such as resentment and revenge, you are only hurting yourself. The person who triggered these emotions has no awareness or hopes you carry the burden. If you want to "win," set the pain free. What old baggage can you release? What micro-wins did you experience? Capture your thoughts, actions and decisions daily.

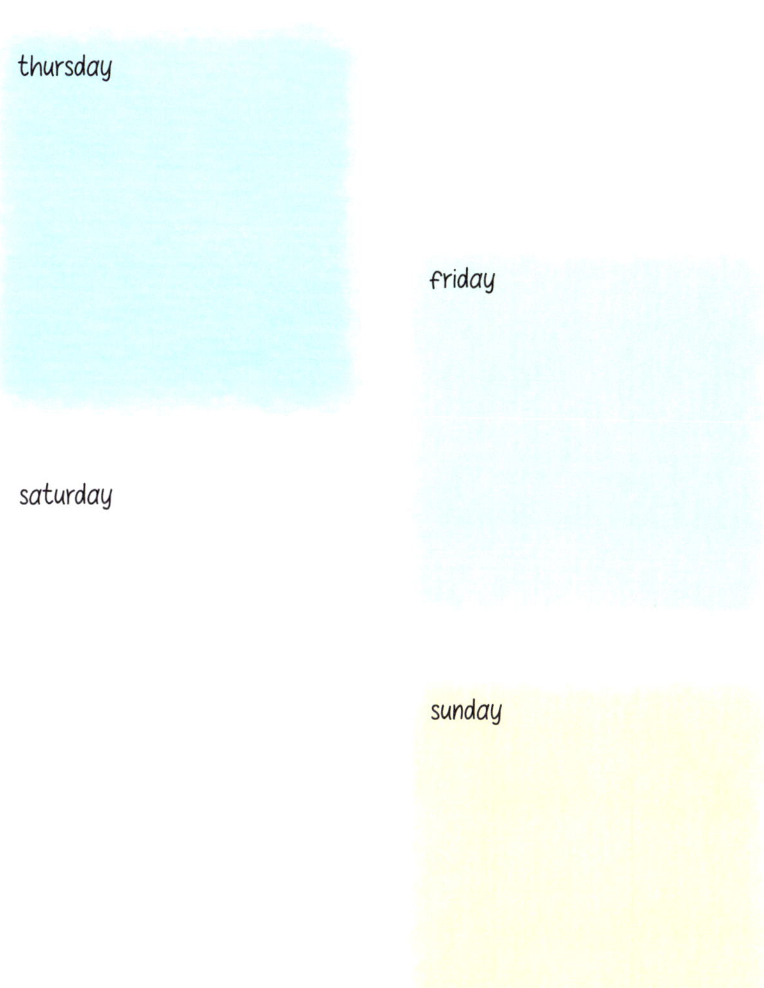

What have you learned about yourself that you can carry forward into the weeks, months, and years to come? What are you ready to let go of so you can live into your best life? Small actions each week will lead to big results.

Well done!

What have you learned about yourself this week? What micro-wins will you celebrate this week? How does it make you feel to acknowledge these achievements?

WEEK TWENTY-THREE

Apologizing is a sign of good character and strength.

An apology can validate you understand social boundaries and may rebuild trust in relationships.

An apology can go a long way towards rebuilding trust and reducing stress. When you take the first step towards mending a relationship, you free yourself of emotional burden and you may make the other person feel good too. Is there anything you may want to apologize for that has been left unsaid? What micro-wins did you experience? Capture your thoughts, actions and decisions daily.

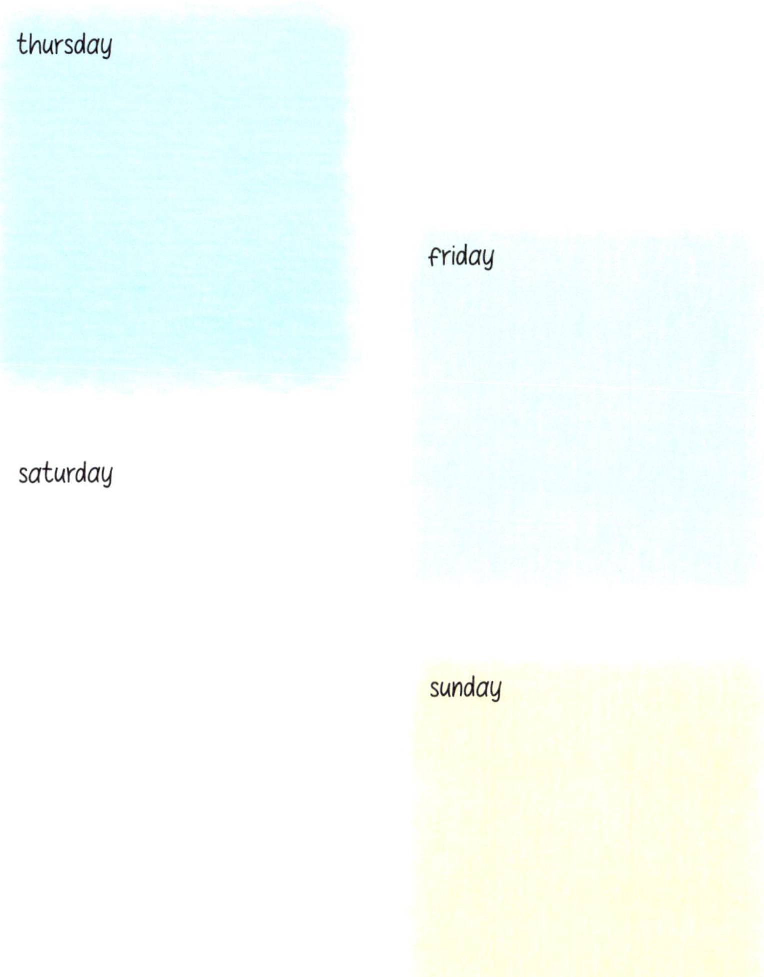

What have you learned about yourself that you can carry forward into the weeks, months, and years to come? What are you ready to let go of so you can live into your best life? Small actions each week will lead to big results.

Well done!

What have you learned about yourself this week? What micro-wins will you celebrate this week? How does it make you feel to acknowledge these achievements?

WEEK TWENTY-FOUR

Take responsibility for your words, thoughts and actions.

When you own what's happening in your life you can shape your future.

monday

tuesday

wednesday

Stop blaming your past circumstances for your current situation. Say what you mean, mean what you say, and follow through on your commitments. These simple ideas will put you in the driver's seat of your life. How are you taking responsibility for your life? What micro-wins did you experience? Capture your thoughts, actions and decisions daily.

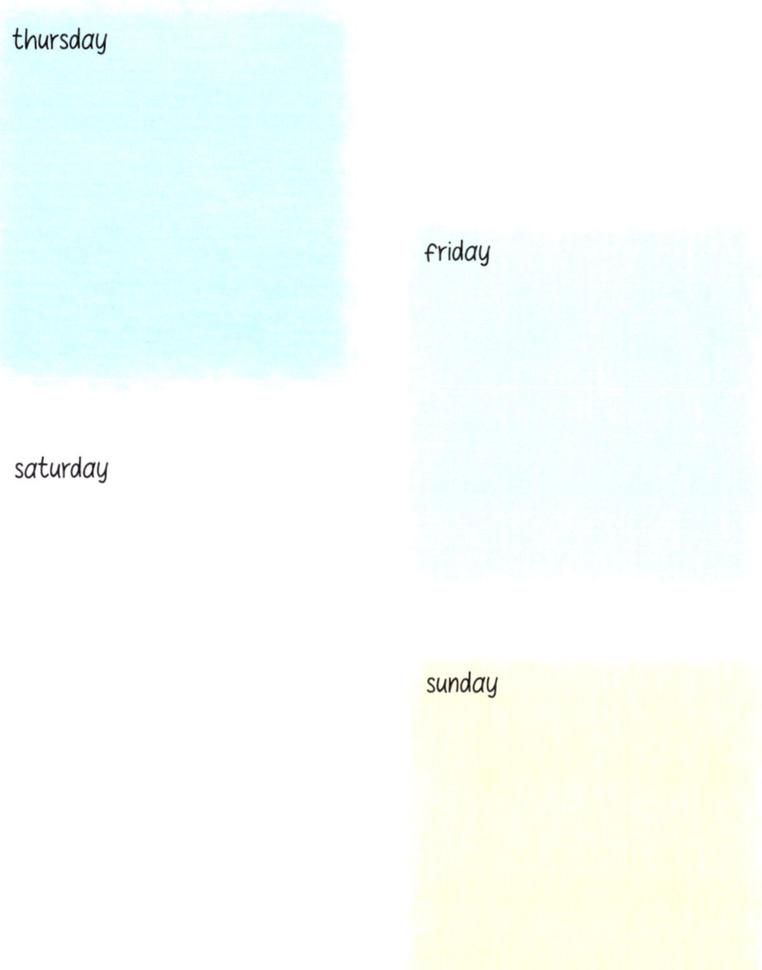

What have you learned about yourself that you can carry forward into the weeks, months, and years to come? What are you ready to let go of so you can live into your best life? Small actions each week will lead to big results.

Well done!

What have you learned about yourself this week? What micro-wins will you celebrate this week? How does it make you feel to acknowledge these achievements?

WEEK TWENTY-FIVE

Each day, make a difference in someone's life.

Random acts of kindness may reduce your stress, make the recipient feel good, and have a ripple effect.

monday

tuesday

wednesday

Through the years, studies have found that kindness is linked to happiness and feeling content. In fact, research shows that each act of kindness may increase your happiness levels. How have you made a difference in the life of someone? What micro-wins did you experience? Capture your thoughts, actions and decisions daily.

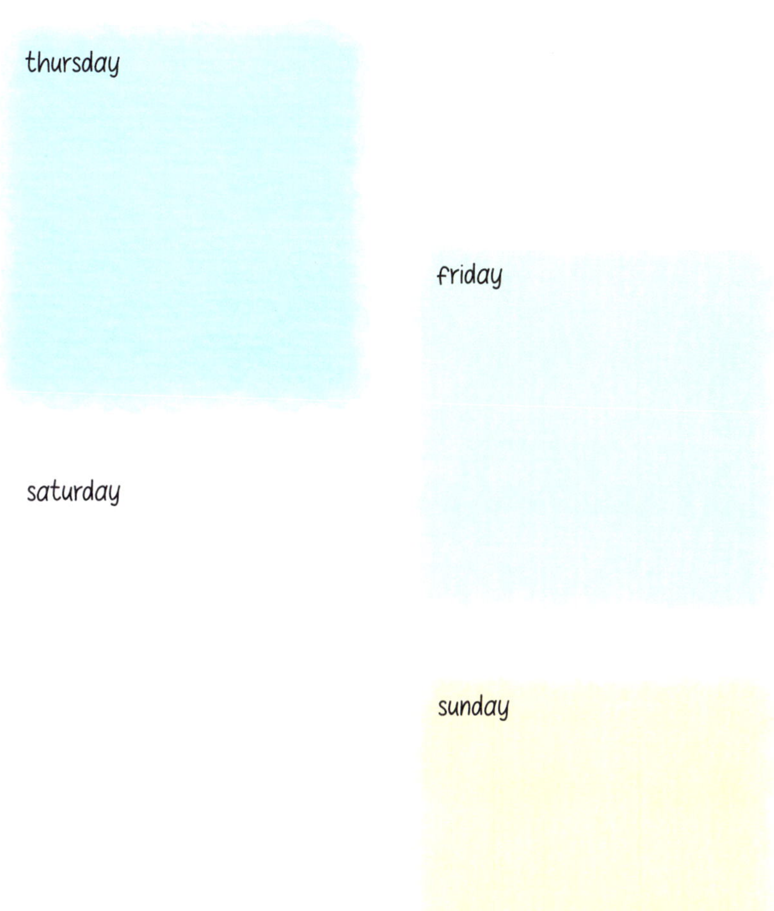

What have you learned about yourself that you can carry forward into the weeks, months, and years to come? What are you ready to let go of so you can live into your best life? Small actions each week will lead to big results.

Well done!

What have you learned about yourself this week? What micro-wins will you celebrate this week? How does it make you feel to acknowledge these achievements?

WEEK TWENTY-SIX

People are mirrors for us.

The people in our lives reflect back to us that which we can learn about ourselves.

monday

tuesday

wednesday

The concept, known as "psychological projection," is a tool for self-awareness. When you observe a trait, behavior or characteristic that elicits a strong emotional response, it may be an attribute you are unaware of in yourself. What have you learned? What micro-wins did you experience? Capture your thoughts, actions and decisions daily.

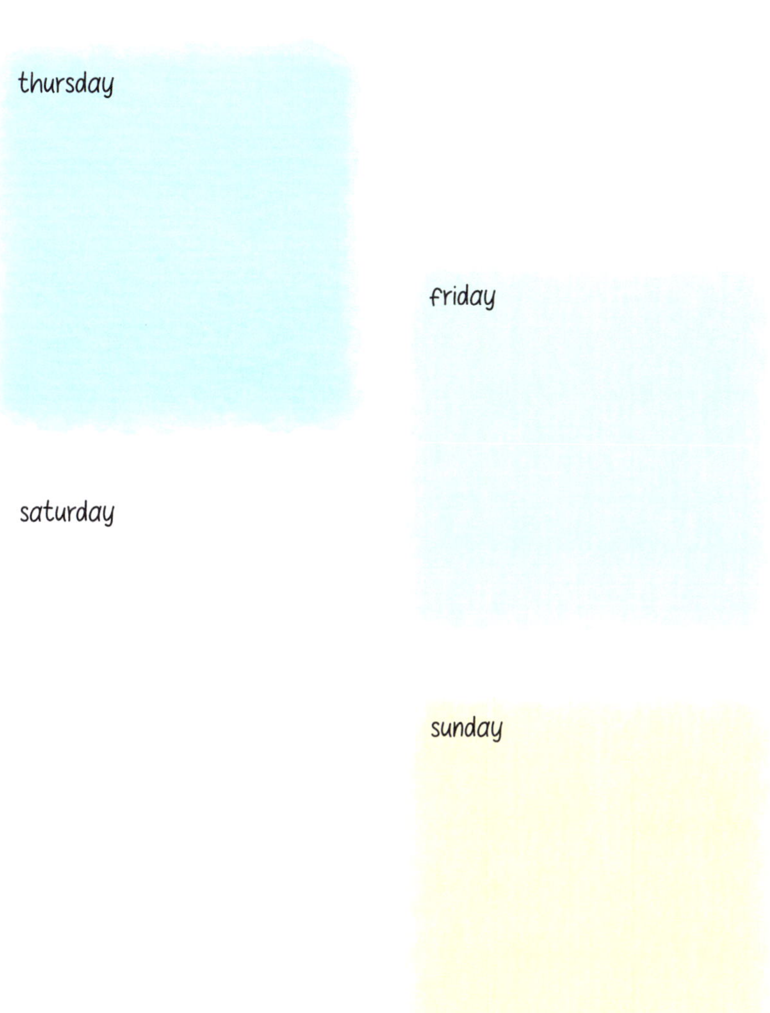

What have you learned about yourself that you can carry forward into the weeks, months, and years to come? What are you ready to let go of so you can live into your best life? Small actions each week will lead to big results.

Well done!

What have you learned about yourself this week? What micro-wins will you celebrate this week? How does it make you feel to acknowledge these achievements?

WEEK TWENTY-SEVEN

When you see brilliance in others, see it as a reflection of your brilliance.

Mirrors don't discriminate. See what you are being shown.

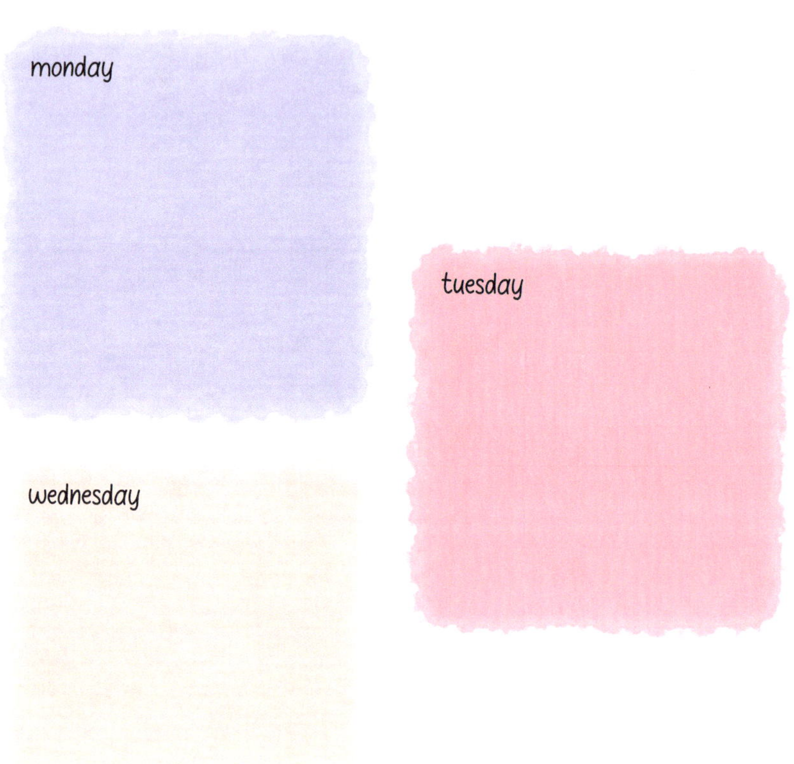

Just as you may notice opportunities for improvement are reflected back to you, people also reflect back to you all the ways you are amazing. What have you noticed in others that you want to see in yourself? How can you bring it to life? What micro-wins did you experience? Capture your thoughts, actions and decisions daily.

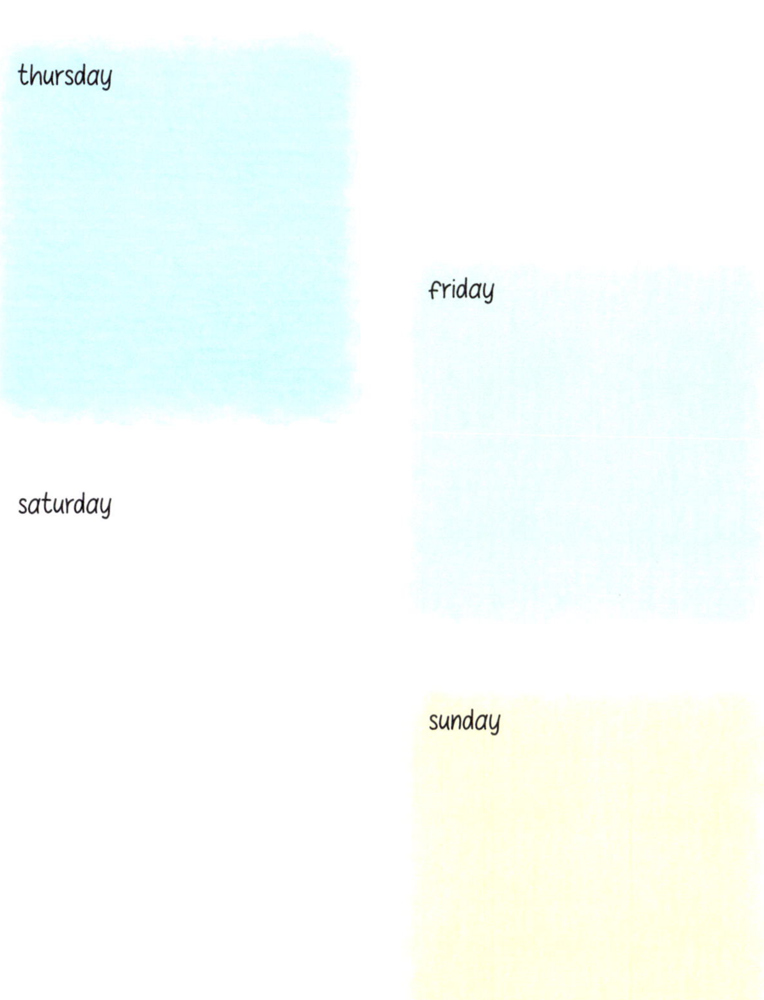

What have you learned about yourself that you can carry forward into the weeks, months, and years to come? What are you ready to let go of so you can live into your best life? Small actions each week will lead to big results.

Well done!

What have you learned about yourself this week? What micro-wins will you celebrate this week? How does it make you feel to acknowledge these achievements?

WEEK TWENTY-EIGHT

Reflect honestly, identify opportunities and take action.

This is a formula for integrating continuous improvement into your life.

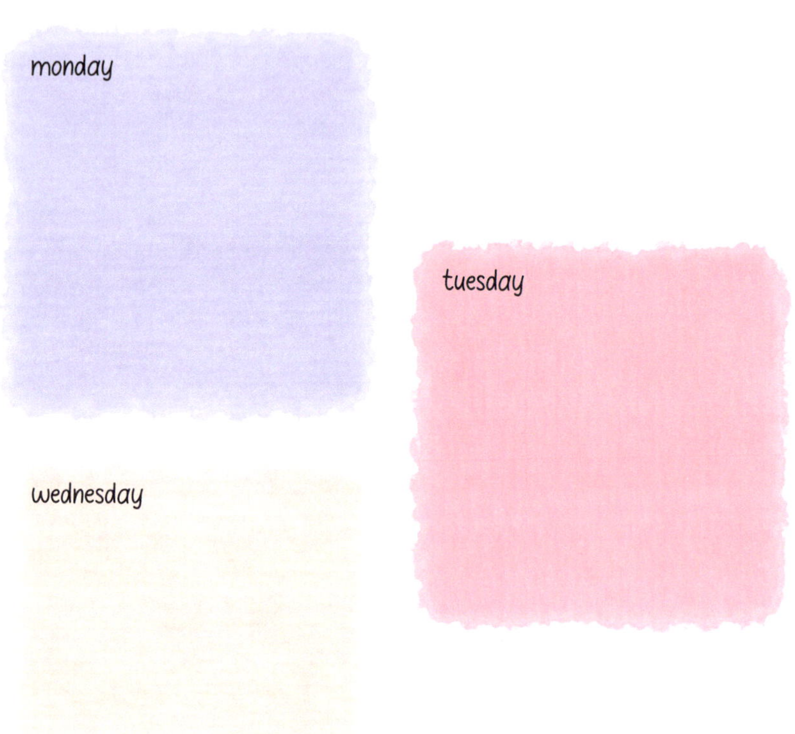

When you start to improve in one area of your life, you naturally begin to feel more fulfilled. Since all areas of your life are integrated, small improvements in one area will have a ripple effect throughout your life. What is one small improvement you can make? What micro-wins did you experience? Capture your thoughts, actions and decisions daily.

thursday

friday

saturday

sunday

What have you learned about yourself that you can carry forward into the weeks, months, and years to come? What are you ready to let go of so you can live into your best life? Small actions each week will lead to big results.

Well done!

What have you learned about yourself this week? What micro-wins will you celebrate this week? How does it make you feel to acknowledge these achievements?

WEEK TWENTY-NINE

W.A.I.T.

Why Am I Talking? You have two ears and one mouth. See what happens when you listen more.

monday

tuesday

wednesday

Everyone loves to talk, and their favorite topic is themselves. When you are engaged in conversation, remember to listen. When you listen to what others are saying and what they are holding back, you learn more about them. What did you learn by listening more? What micro-wins did you experience? Capture your thoughts, actions and decisions daily.

thursday

friday

saturday

sunday

What have you learned about yourself that you can carry forward into the weeks, months, and years to come? What are you ready to let go of so you can live into your best life? Small actions each week will lead to big results.

Well done!

What have you learned about yourself this week? What micro-wins will you celebrate this week? How does it make you feel to acknowledge these achievements?

WEEK THIRTY

Ask more questions.

People love to talk about themselves, so ask questions to learn more.

monday

tuesday

wednesday

Since people love to talk about themselves, help them out by asking questions. When you ask thought-provoking questions, people will feel you are interested in them, and they will share more. What questions give you the most intriguing responses? What micro-wins did you experience? Capture your thoughts, actions and decisions daily.

thursday

friday

saturday

sunday

What have you learned about yourself that you can carry forward into the weeks, months, and years to come? What are you ready to let go of so you can live into your best life? Small actions each week will lead to big results.

Well done!

What have you learned about yourself this week? What micro-wins will you celebrate this week? How does it make you feel to acknowledge these achievements?

WEEK THIRTY-ONE

Be curious.

When you are curious, you open your mind to learning and seeing an abundance of possibilities.

monday

tuesday

wednesday

Peter Drucker's philosophy for being "intelligently" curious can help you expand your perspective and lead to greater success in all areas of your life. What are you curious about and what have you learned? What micro-wins did you experience? Capture your thoughts, actions and decisions daily.

thursday

friday

saturday

sunday

What have you learned about yourself that you can carry forward into the weeks, months, and years to come? What are you ready to let go of so you can live into your best life? Small actions each week will lead to big results.

Well done!

What have you learned about yourself this week? What micro-wins will you celebrate this week? How does it make you feel to acknowledge these achievements?

WEEK THIRTY-TWO

It's not about you, it's about them.

When things don't make sense, it's likely the situation has nothing to do with you.

monday

tuesday

wednesday

While it's important to take responsibility for yourself, there may be times when a situation or something someone says makes no sense to you. This is often an indication that it's more about the others involved than you. What do you notice when you allow the responsibility to lie with those it's intended? What micro-wins did you experience? Capture your thoughts, actions and decisions daily.

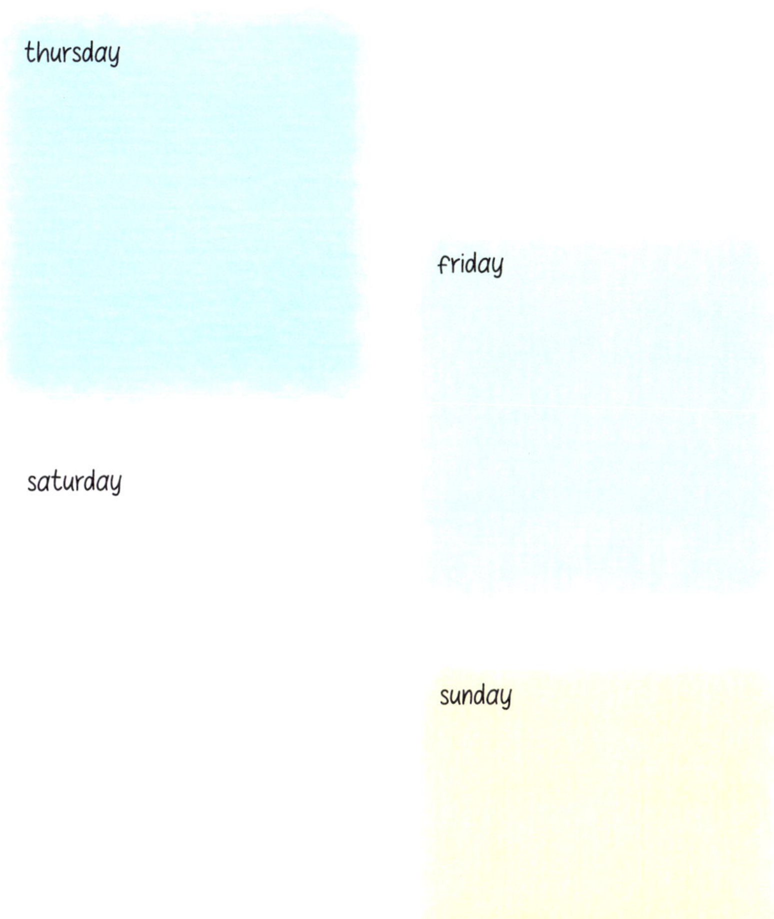

What have you learned about yourself that you can carry forward into the weeks, months, and years to come? What are you ready to let go of so you can live into your best life? Small actions each week will lead to big results.

Well done!

What have you learned about yourself this week? What micro-wins will you celebrate this week? How does it make you feel to acknowledge these achievements?

WEEK THIRTY-THREE

"Let go of what has served its purpose to make room for new opportunities."

~ Paulie Skaja

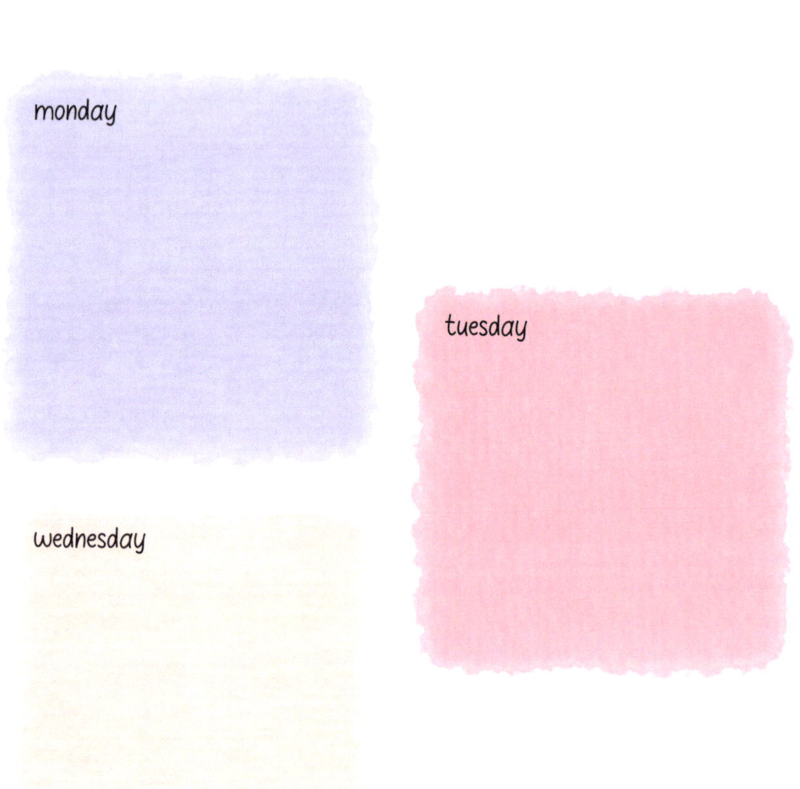

We often hold on to the past out of nostalgia, habit, or because we are unaware that we are. Take an inventory of your life and notice what you are holding onto that is costing you more time, energy or resources than you get in return. What can you let go of to create space for more opportunities? What micro-wins did you experience? Capture your thoughts, actions and decisions daily.

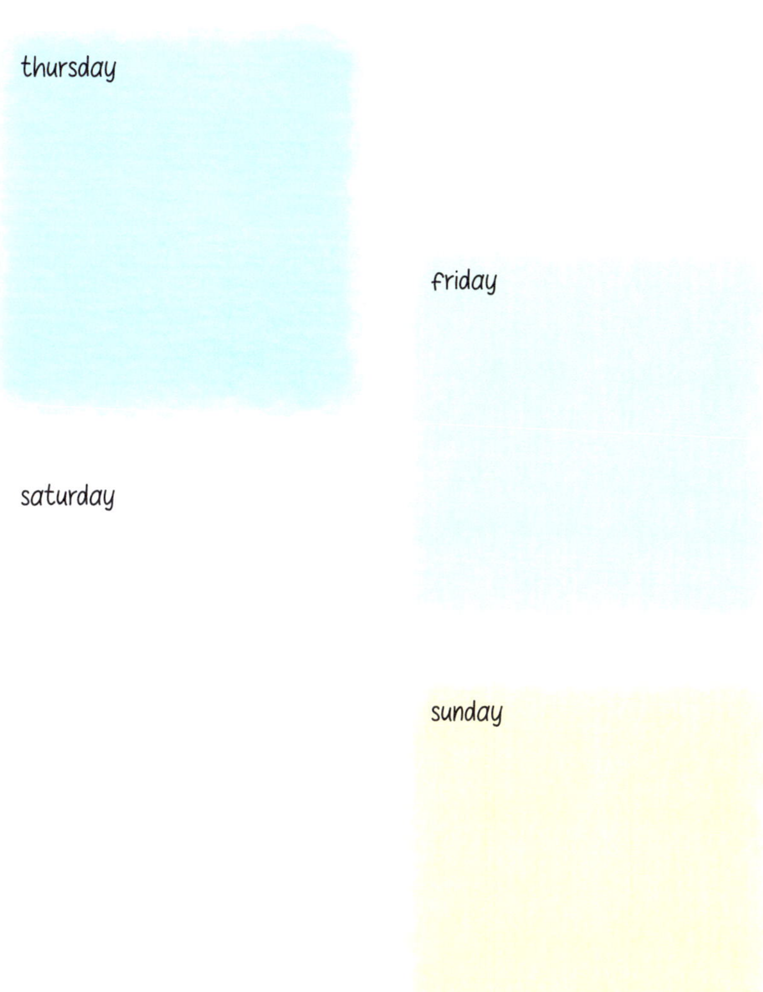

What have you learned about yourself that you can carry forward into the weeks, months, and years to come? What are you ready to let go of so you can live into your best life? Small actions each week will lead to big results.

Well done!

What have you learned about yourself this week? What micro-wins will you celebrate this week? How does it make you feel to acknowledge these achievements?

WEEK THIRTY-FOUR

"Be open to the possibilities, they are everywhere."

~ Paulie Skaja

monday

tuesday

wednesday

When you are open to new ideas and new experiences, your potential expands. Ask questions. Be curious. Notice what new ideas and information presents itself. What possibilities do you see? What micro-wins did you experience? Capture your thoughts, actions and decisions daily.

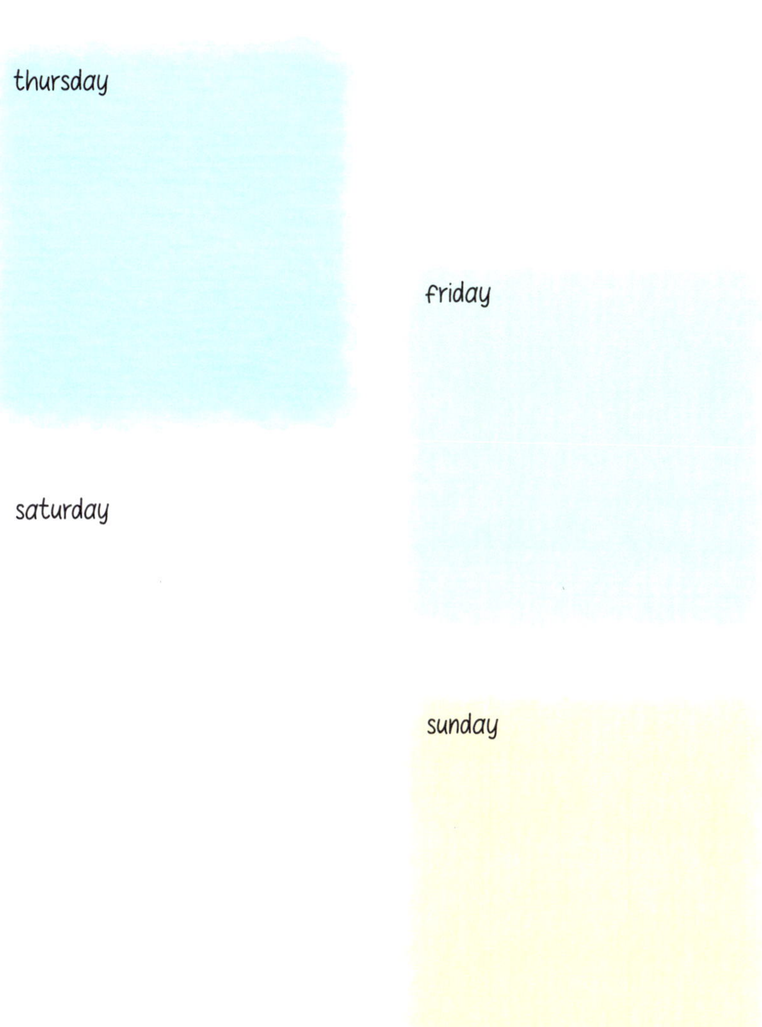

What have you learned about yourself that you can carry forward into the weeks, months, and years to come? What are you ready to let go of so you can live into your best life? Small actions each week will lead to big results.

Well done!

What have you learned about yourself this week? What micro-wins will you celebrate this week? How does it make you feel to acknowledge these achievements?

WEEK THIRTY-FIVE

"It's kind of fun to do the impossible."

~ Walt Disney

monday

tuesday

wednesday

We are only limited by our imaginations. Walt Disney was known for acting on his creative ideas. What in your life has seemed impossible and how can it become possible? What micro-wins did you experience? Capture your thoughts, actions and decisions daily.

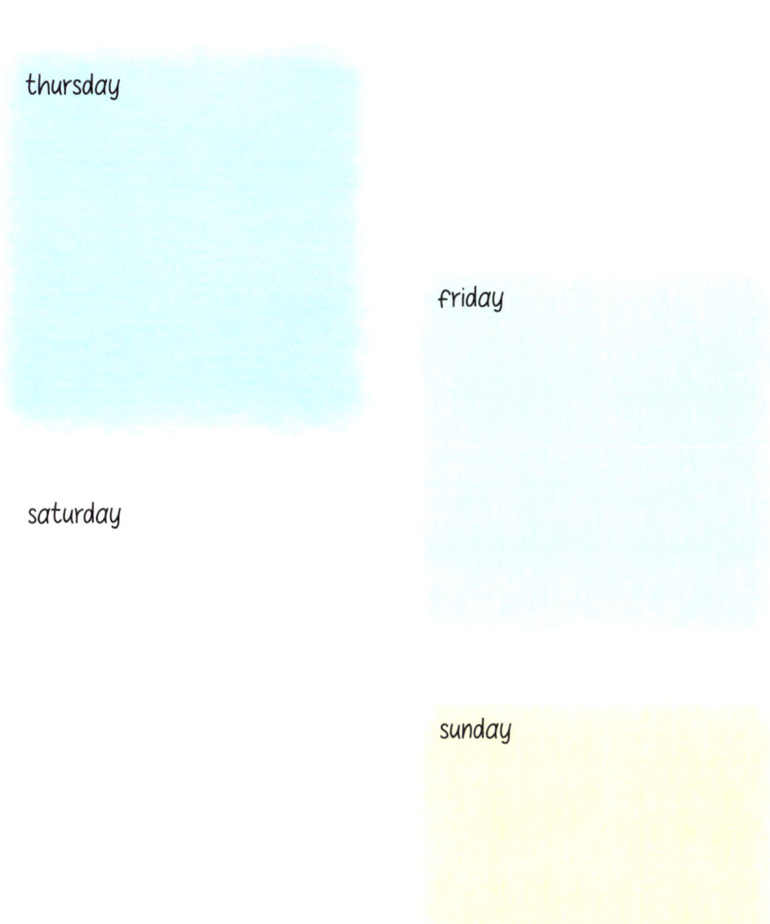

What have you learned about yourself that you can carry forward into the weeks, months, and years to come? What are you ready to let go of so you can live into your best life? Small actions each week will lead to big results.

Well done!

What have you learned about yourself this week? What micro-wins will you celebrate this week? How does it make you feel to acknowledge these achievements?

WEEK THIRTY-SIX

Believing is seeing.

Our beliefs play a strong part in how we see the circumstances and situations in our life.

monday

tuesday

wednesday

When you believe something to be true, your RAS will find proof you are correct. Notice what you are believing about yourself and your situation. What beliefs need to change for you to see proof that you are moving towards your goals? What micro-wins did you experience? Capture your thoughts, actions and decisions daily.

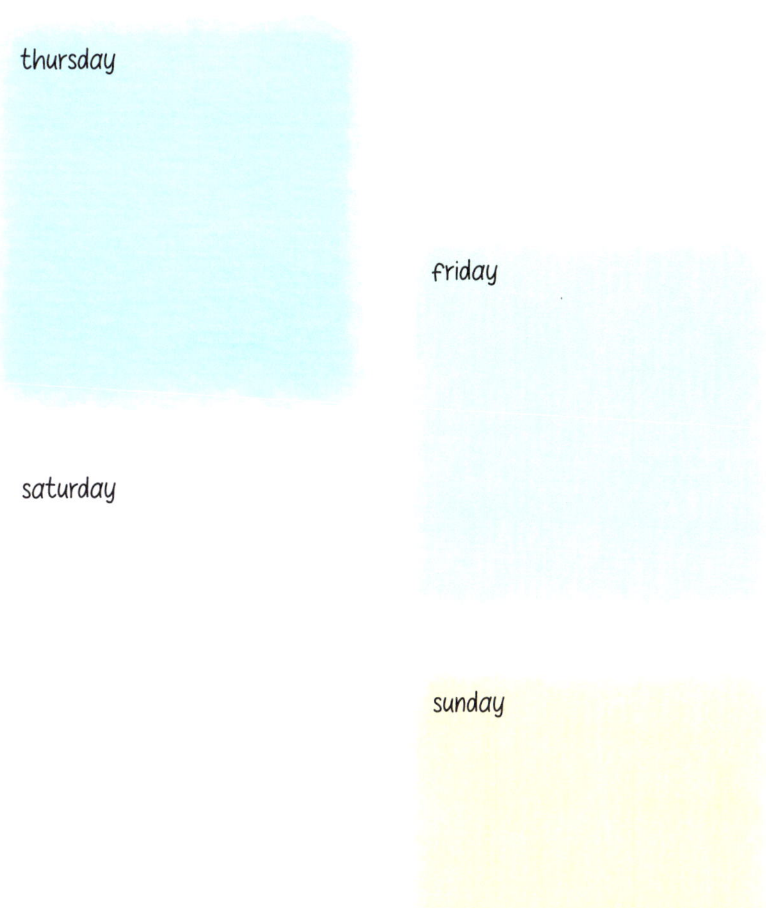

What have you learned about yourself that you can carry forward into the weeks, months, and years to come? What are you ready to let go of so you can live into your best life? Small actions each week will lead to big results.

Well done!

What have you learned about yourself this week? What micro-wins will you celebrate this week? How does it make you feel to acknowledge these achievements?

WEEK THIRTY-SEVEN

"Courage is not about knowing the path. It is about taking the first step."

~ Katie J. Davis

monday

tuesday

wednesday

They say the most difficult part of a journey is the first step. When you decide to do something, that is the first step. The next step is to do it. Imagine you have the courage to create your dream life. What steps do you take? What micro-wins did you experience? Capture your thoughts, actions and decisions daily.

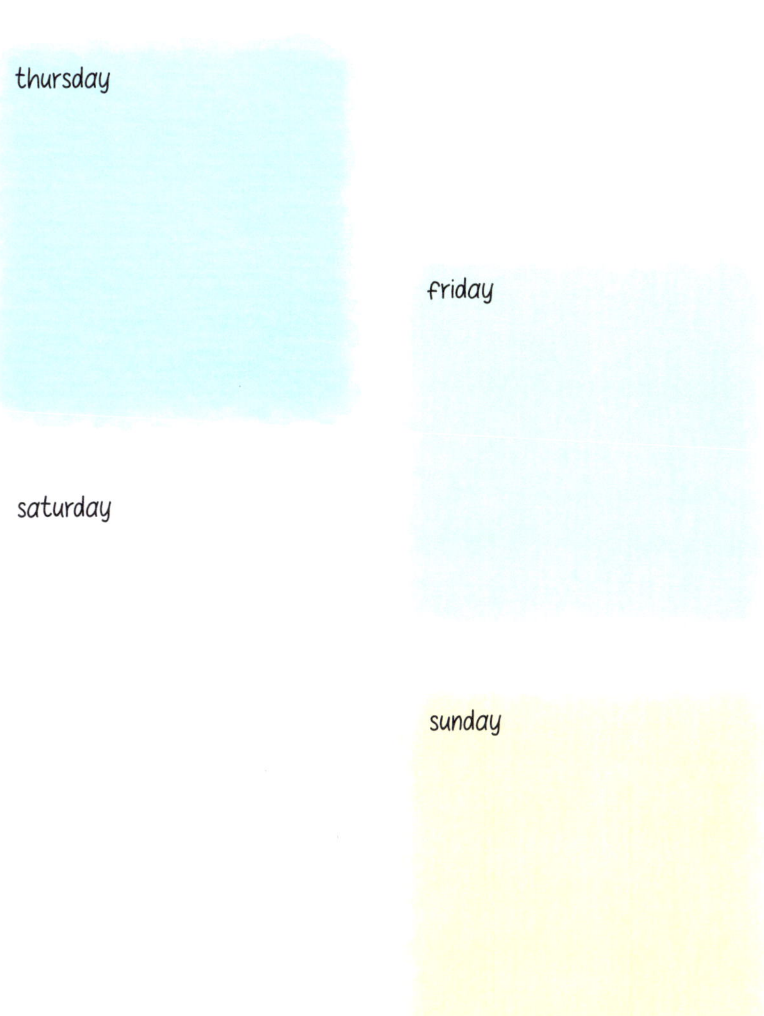

What have you learned about yourself that you can carry forward into the weeks, months, and years to come? What are you ready to let go of so you can live into your best life? Small actions each week will lead to big results.

Well done!

What have you learned about yourself this week? What micro-wins will you celebrate this week? How does it make you feel to acknowledge these achievements?

WEEK THIRTY-EIGHT

Learn from the past and move forward.

98% of your thoughts today are the same thoughts you had yesterday.

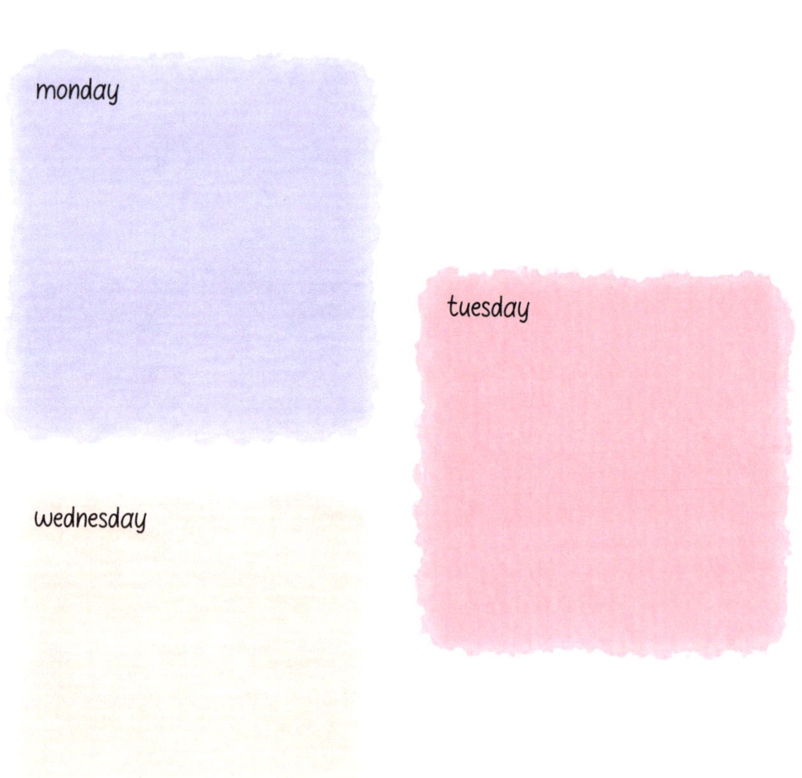

You average between 50,000 and 70,000 thoughts each day; however, about 98% of these thoughts are the same thoughts you had yesterday. Which thoughts can you learn from and let go? Which are holding you back from achieving your goals? What purpose do they serve? What micro-wins did you experience? Capture your thoughts, actions and decisions daily.

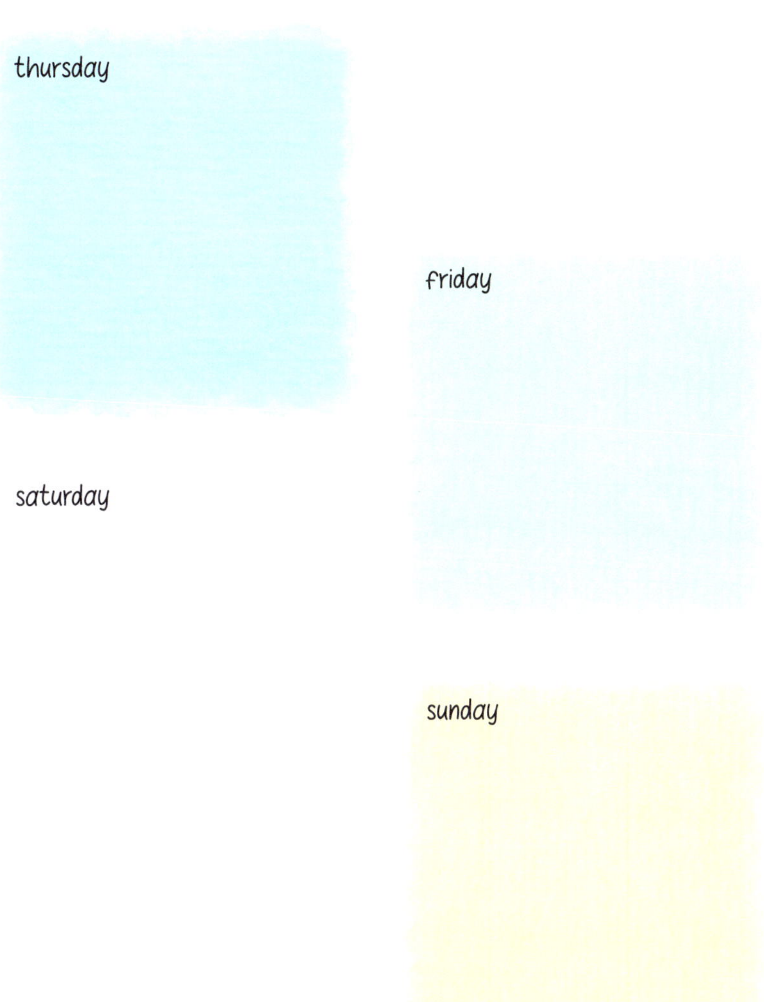

What have you learned about yourself that you can carry forward into the weeks, months, and years to come? What are you ready to let go of so you can live into your best life? Small actions each week will lead to big results.

Well done!

What have you learned about yourself this week? What micro-wins will you celebrate this week? How does it make you feel to acknowledge these achievements?

WEEK THIRTY-NINE

Loss and failure lead to wisdom and knowledge.

When things don't go as planned, the result provides an opportunity to learn and grow, if you choose.

monday

tuesday

wednesday

While being successful feels good, it often comes from practice, failure, and trying something different. The more open you are to learning from experiences that don't go as you had hoped, the more wisdom and knowledge you gather for the future. What wisdom have you gleaned? What micro-wins did you experience? Capture your thoughts, actions and decisions daily.

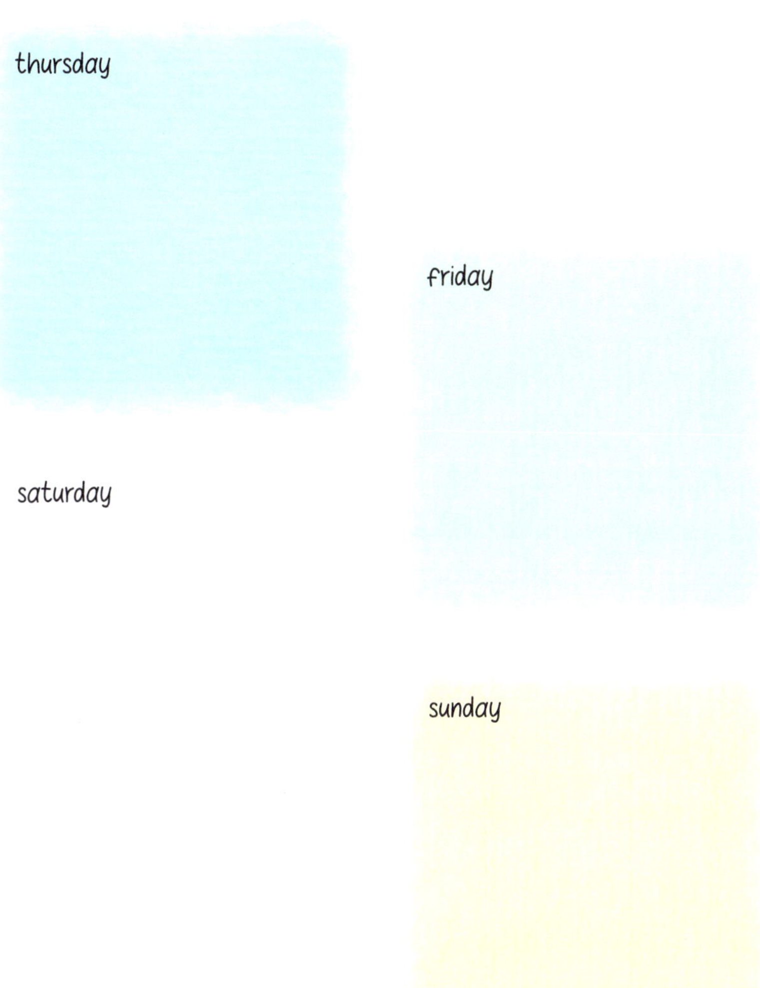

What have you learned about yourself that you can carry forward into the weeks, months, and years to come? What are you ready to let go of so you can live into your best life? Small actions each week will lead to big results.

Well done!

What have you learned about yourself this week? What micro-wins will you celebrate this week? How does it make you feel to acknowledge these achievements?

WEEK FORTY

"It's ok to let go of perfection… good enough is perfect."

~ Paulie Skaja

monday

tuesday

wednesday

Perfectionism is fueled by the fear of making a mistake or not being good enough. Chances are, you are more amazing in the eyes of others than you can imagine. What in your life is good enough? What micro-wins did you experience? Capture your thoughts, actions and decisions daily.

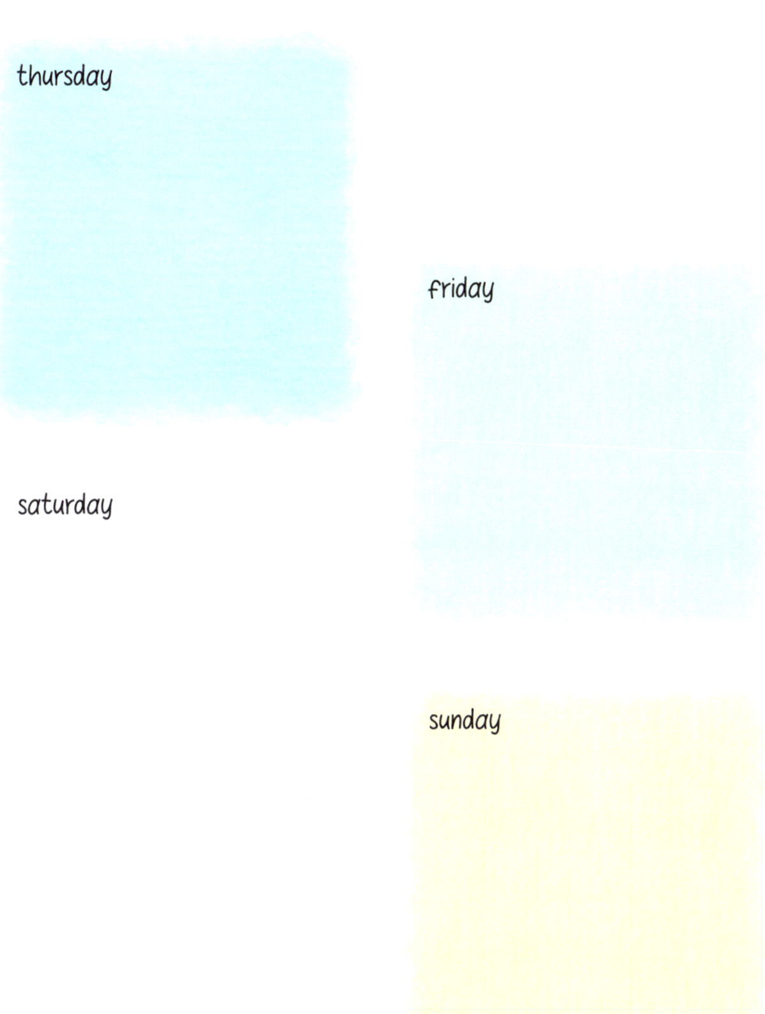

What have you learned about yourself that you can carry forward into the weeks, months, and years to come? What are you ready to let go of so you can live into your best life? Small actions each week will lead to big results.

Well done!

What have you learned about yourself this week? What micro-wins will you celebrate this week? How does it make you feel to acknowledge these achievements?

WEEK FORTY-ONE

Live your life with integrity.

When you are honest and follow a strong moral compass, it is easier to live your life fully.

monday

tuesday

wednesday

Living in integrity is linked to your self-esteem, happiness, and success in all areas of your life. It takes self-reflection, accountability, and courage and it means others can trust you and respect you. How are you living in integrity? What micro-wins did you experience? Capture your thoughts, actions and decisions daily.

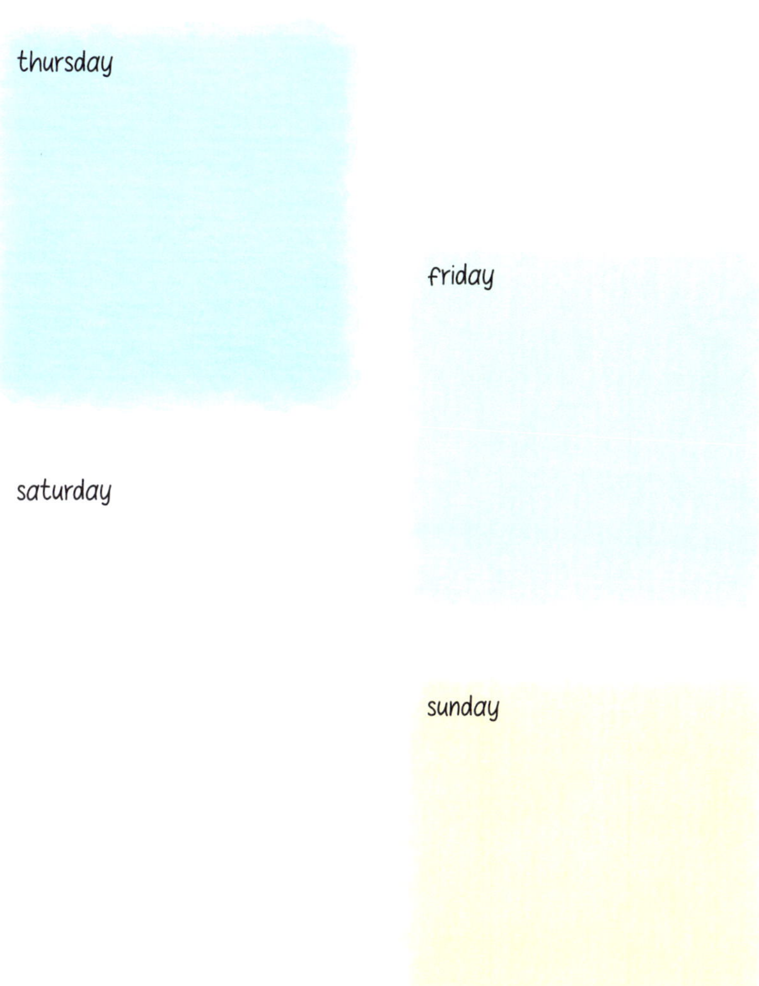

What have you learned about yourself that you can carry forward into the weeks, months, and years to come? What are you ready to let go of so you can live into your best life? Small actions each week will lead to big results.

Well done!

What have you learned about yourself this week? What micro-wins will you celebrate this week? How does it make you feel to acknowledge these achievements?

WEEK FORTY-TWO

It's ok to change your mind.

In fact, if you don't, perhaps you aren't really living into your best life.

monday

tuesday

wednesday

Throughout any given day, you change your mind often. Perhaps you wanted coffee and then decided on tea or planned to go right and then turned left. You change your mind to align with new information. What decisions have you made that you may want to change your mind about and why? What micro-wins did you experience? Capture your thoughts, actions and decisions daily.

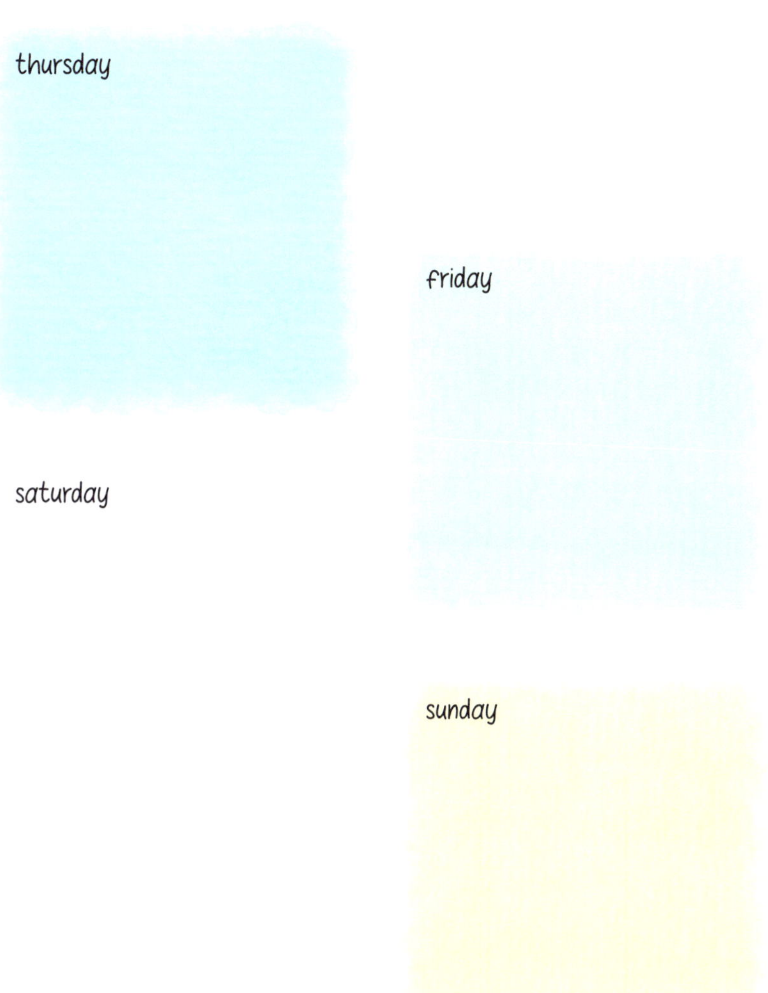

What have you learned about yourself that you can carry forward into the weeks, months, and years to come? What are you ready to let go of so you can live into your best life? Small actions each week will lead to big results.

Well done!

What have you learned about yourself this week? What micro-wins will you celebrate this week? How does it make you feel to acknowledge these achievements?

WEEK FORTY-THREE

"Just because others think it, doesn't mean you need to believe it. Create your own path."

– Paulie Skaja

monday

tuesday

wednesday

Often, well-meaning people have ideas about how they think you should live your life. It is YOUR life. Consider what is true for you and let your path unfold. What part of your path are you living based on what others believe? Does this align with your dreams? What micro-wins did you experience? Capture your thoughts, actions and decisions daily.

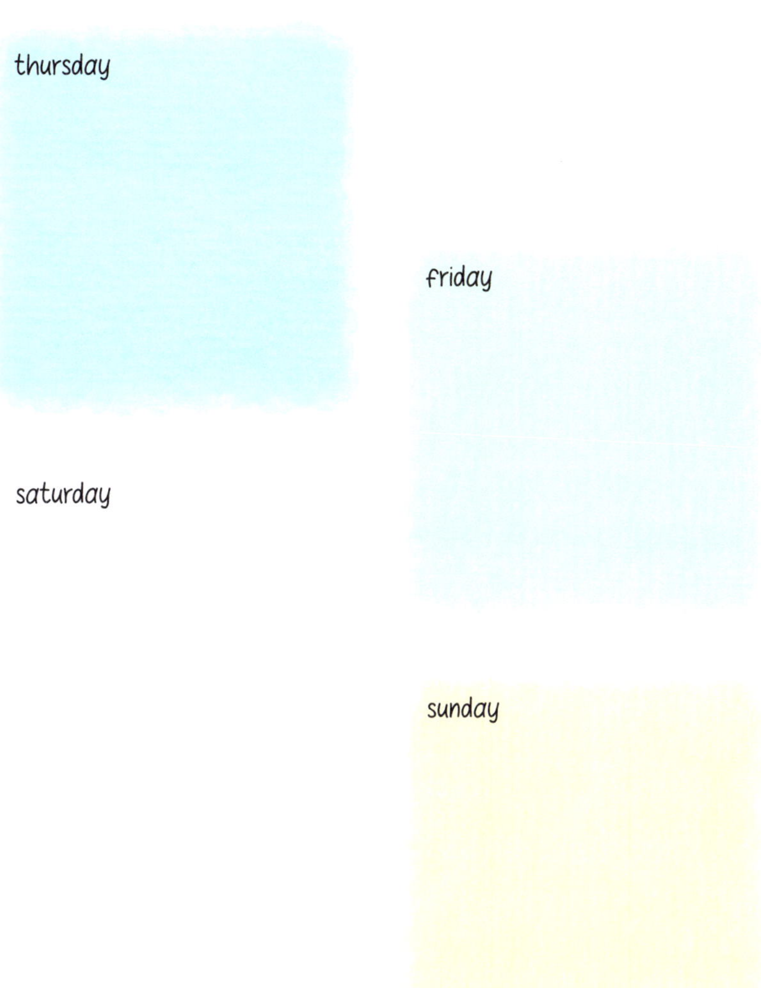

What have you learned about yourself that you can carry forward into the weeks, months, and years to come? What are you ready to let go of so you can live into your best life? Small actions each week will lead to big results.

Well done!

What have you learned about yourself this week? What micro-wins will you celebrate this week? How does it make you feel to acknowledge these achievements?

WEEK FORTY-FOUR

You cannot give to others if you are empty.

Imagine a pyramid of teacups. When you fill the top cup, the extra flows over to the others. This is true in life too.

monday

tuesday

wednesday

Many people push themselves until they have given so much, they feel depleted. This behavior can lead to burnout. Reflect upon your life and consider if there are areas where you are giving too much of yourself. How might you pull back so other people can step up? What micro-wins did you experience? Capture your thoughts, actions and decisions daily.

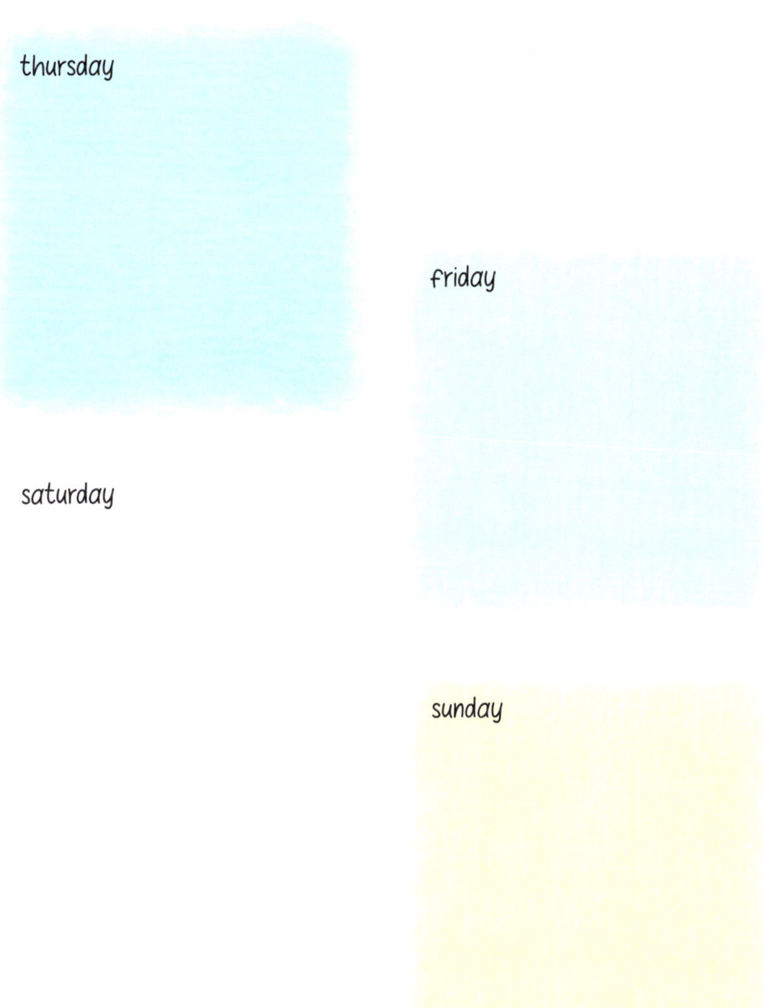

What have you learned about yourself that you can carry forward into the weeks, months, and years to come? What are you ready to let go of so you can live into your best life? Small actions each week will lead to big results.

Well done!

What have you learned about yourself this week? What micro-wins will you celebrate this week? How does it make you feel to acknowledge these achievements?

WEEK FORTY-FIVE

Live with empathy, understanding, and compassion.

We can never really know what someone else is going through but we can strive to understand.

monday

tuesday

wednesday

There is no way you can completely understand what someone else is going through. Rather than judging them, perhaps you can try empathy, compassion, and kindness. When did you judge a person and how might a shift in your view alter your perception? What micro-wins did you experience? Capture your thoughts, actions and decisions daily.

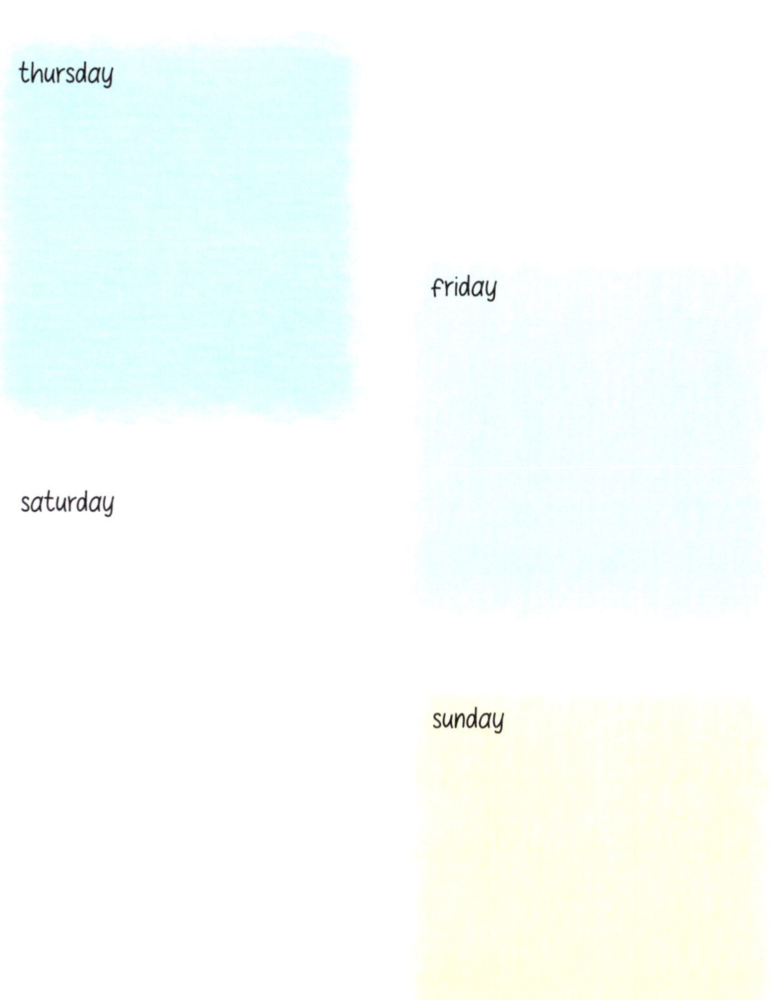

What have you learned about yourself that you can carry forward into the weeks, months, and years to come? What are you ready to let go of so you can live into your best life? Small actions each week will lead to big results.

Well done!

What have you learned about yourself this week? What micro-wins will you celebrate this week? How does it make you feel to acknowledge these achievements?

WEEK FORTY-SIX

"You have a treasure within you that is infinitely greater than anything the world can offer."

– Eckhart Tolle

monday

tuesday

wednesday

Re-read that statement and let it sink in for a moment. You have an infinite number of gifts, talents and skills within you. We all do. What talents have you been hiding that are ready to be shared? What micro-wins did you experience? Capture your thoughts, actions and decisions daily.

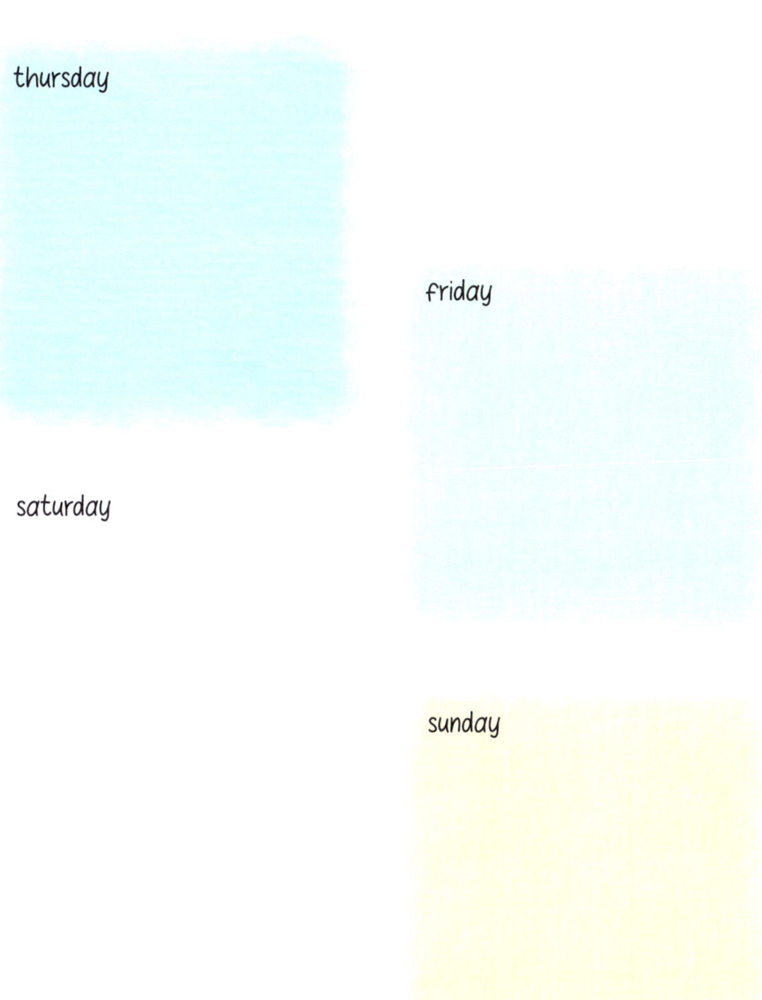

What have you learned about yourself that you can carry forward into the weeks, months, and years to come? What are you ready to let go of so you can live into your best life? Small actions each week will lead to big results.

Well done!

What have you learned about yourself this week? What micro-wins will you celebrate this week? How does it make you feel to acknowledge these achievements?

WEEK FORTY-SEVEN

What got you here won't get you there.

If you keep doing what you've always done, you will get the same results you've always gotten.

When you begin a journey, you go from one point to the next. In order to continue on, you cannot repeat the steps, or you will just be walking in a circle. How are you walking in a circle? What changes can you make to move forward? What micro-wins did you experience? Capture your thoughts, actions and decisions daily.

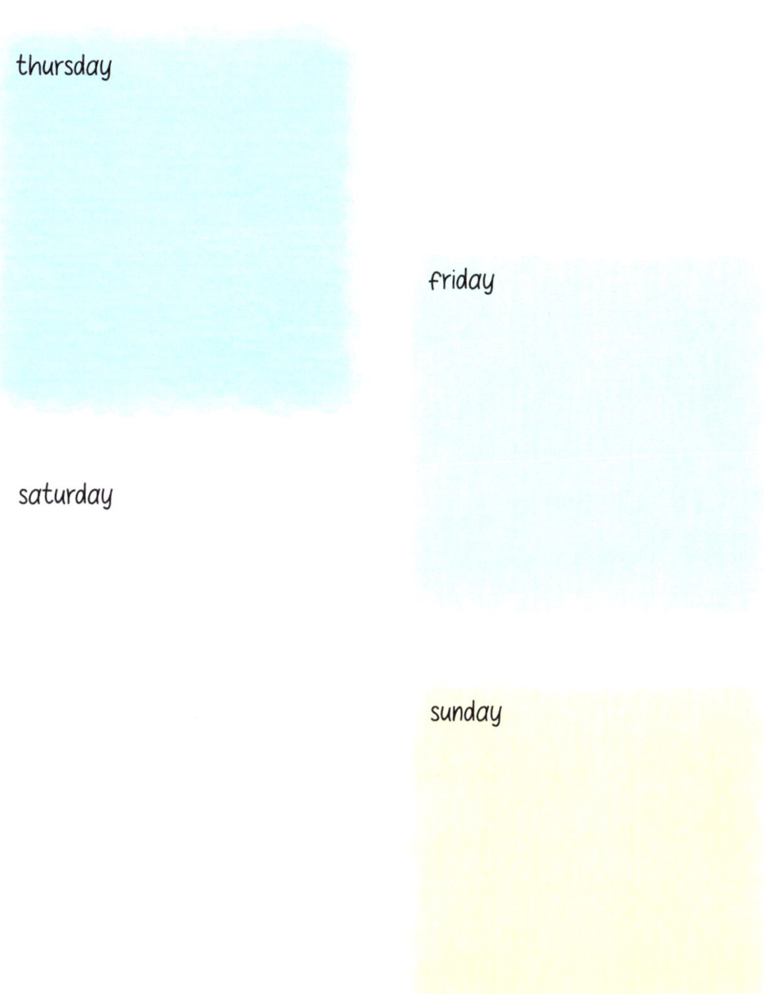

What have you learned about yourself that you can carry forward into the weeks, months, and years to come? What are you ready to let go of so you can live into your best life? Small actions each week will lead to big results.

Well done!

What have you learned about yourself this week? What micro-wins will you celebrate this week? How does it make you feel to acknowledge these achievements?

WEEK FORTY-EIGHT

Inspiration is everywhere.

Close your eyes, think of a question, open your eyes, notice how the first thing you see may help offer the answer.

monday

tuesday

wednesday

Whether you are seeking answers or looking for a new perspective, by allowing yourself to see the world from a new view it will provide you with inspiration. What inspiration can you find each day? What micro-wins did you experience? Capture your thoughts, actions and decisions daily.

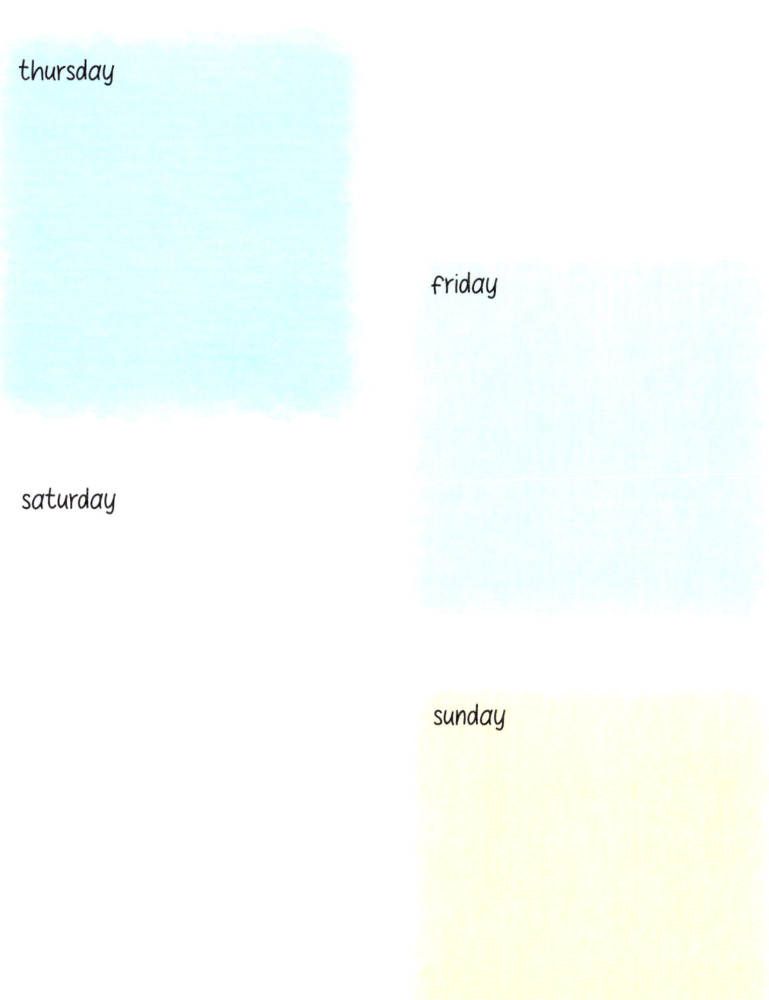

What have you learned about yourself that you can carry forward into the weeks, months, and years to come? What are you ready to let go of so you can live into your best life? Small actions each week will lead to big results.

Well done!

What have you learned about yourself this week? What micro-wins will you celebrate this week? How does it make you feel to acknowledge these achievements?

WEEK FORTY-NINE

How you see anything is how you see everything.

If you want things to change, alter how you see them and make choices based on your new perspective.

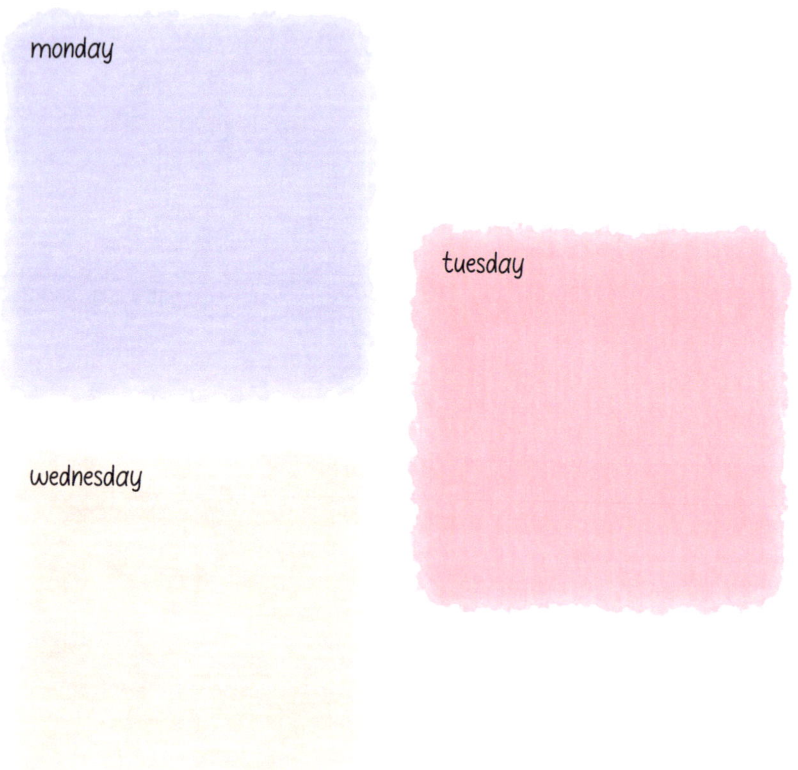

Perhaps you see the glass as half full and observe possibilities everywhere. Maybe you're a realist and take life at face value or a pessimist who is always expecting the worst. How might you shift your view to gain new perspectives? What micro-wins did you experience? Capture your thoughts, actions and decisions daily.

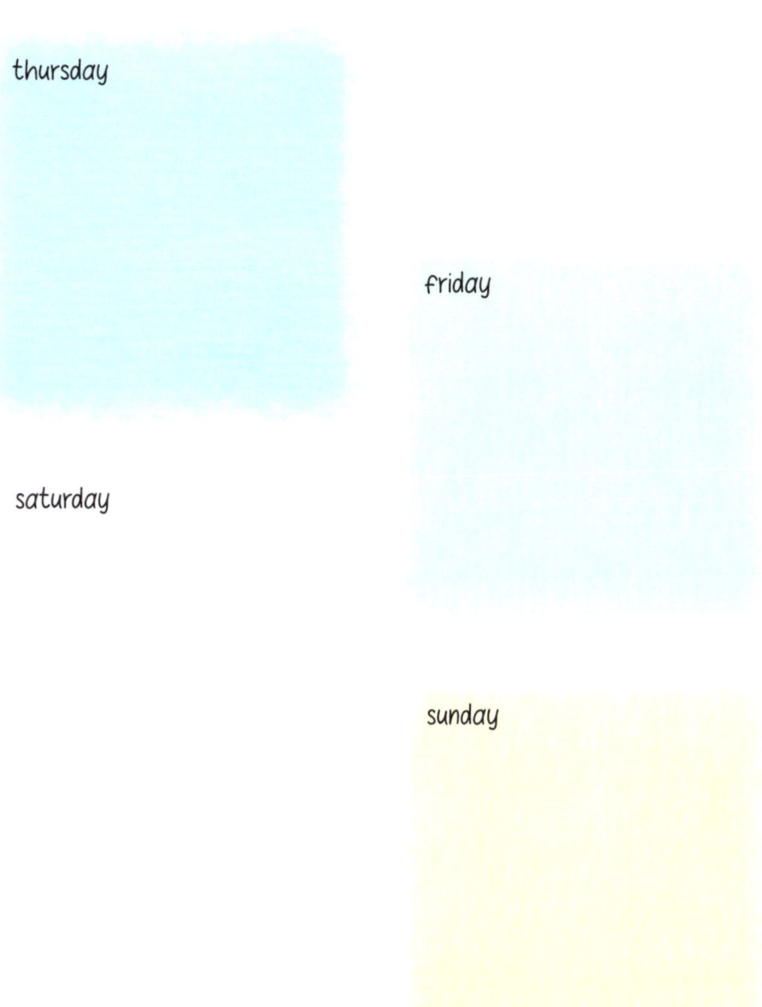

What have you learned about yourself that you can carry forward into the weeks, months, and years to come? What are you ready to let go of so you can live into your best life? Small actions each week will lead to big results.

Well done!

What have you learned about yourself this week? What micro-wins will you celebrate this week? How does it make you feel to acknowledge these achievements?

WEEK FIFTY

Choose one thing you would like to improve in your life.

Do that thing every day for one week. Notice how things have changed. Do something new next week.

monday

tuesday

wednesday

When you focus your energy on doing one thing, you will begin to see progress relatively quickly. If you keep doing that thing and build on it, you will see a broader spectrum of improvement. What is one thing you can focus on improving this week? What micro-wins did you experience? Capture your thoughts, actions and decisions daily.

thursday

friday

saturday

sunday

What have you learned about yourself that you can carry forward into the weeks, months, and years to come? What are you ready to let go of so you can live into your best life? Small actions each week will lead to big results.

Well done!

What have you learned about yourself this week? What micro-wins will you celebrate this week? How does it make you feel to acknowledge these achievements?

WEEK FIFTY-ONE

Integrate continuous improvement into your life.

1% improvement daily leads to becoming 37 times better in just one year.

monday

tuesday

wednesday

Small, incremental improvements lead to significant results. When you choose to make small changes and build upon the activity daily, you will achieve your goals faster. What can you improve each day? What micro-wins did you experience? Capture your thoughts, actions and decisions daily.

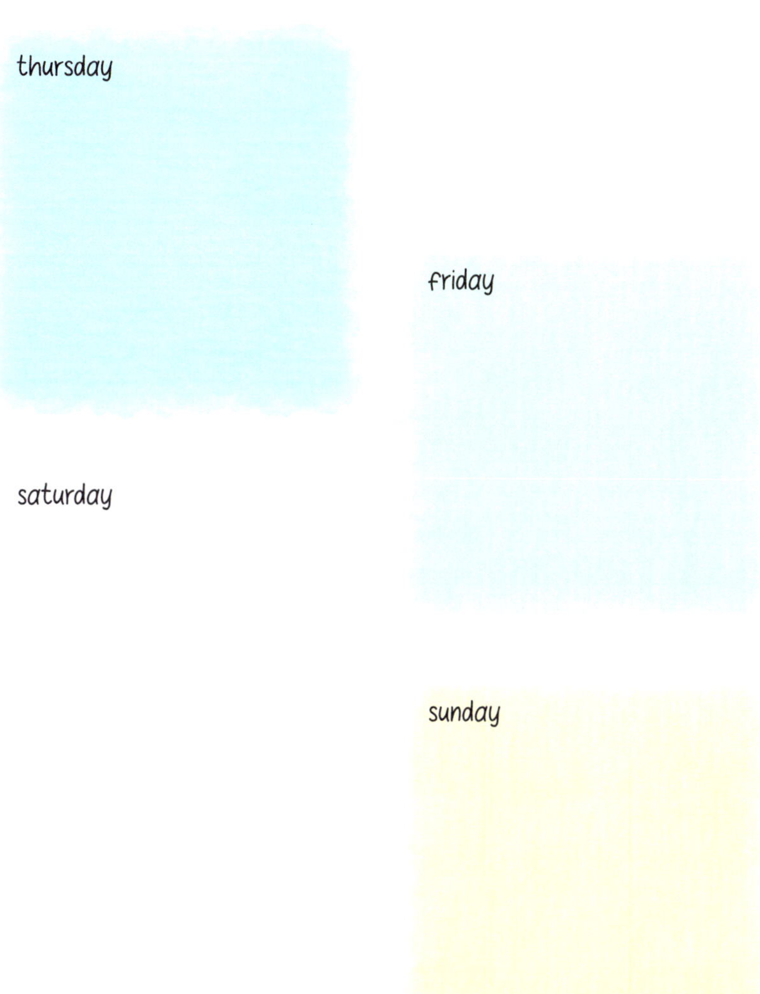

What have you learned about yourself that you can carry forward into the weeks, months, and years to come? What are you ready to let go of so you can live into your best life? Small actions each week will lead to big results.

Well done!

What have you learned about yourself this week? What micro-wins will you celebrate this week? How does it make you feel to acknowledge these achievements?

WEEK FIFTY-TWO

Give yourself some grace.

You are only human Show yourself kindness and self-compassion and notice the difference.

monday

tuesday

wednesday

We tend to be our own worst critic. Notice your thoughts. Are these the words you would say to a friend? If not, show yourself some kindness and notice what changes. When might you be gentler with yourself? What micro-wins did you experience? Capture your thoughts, actions and decisions daily.

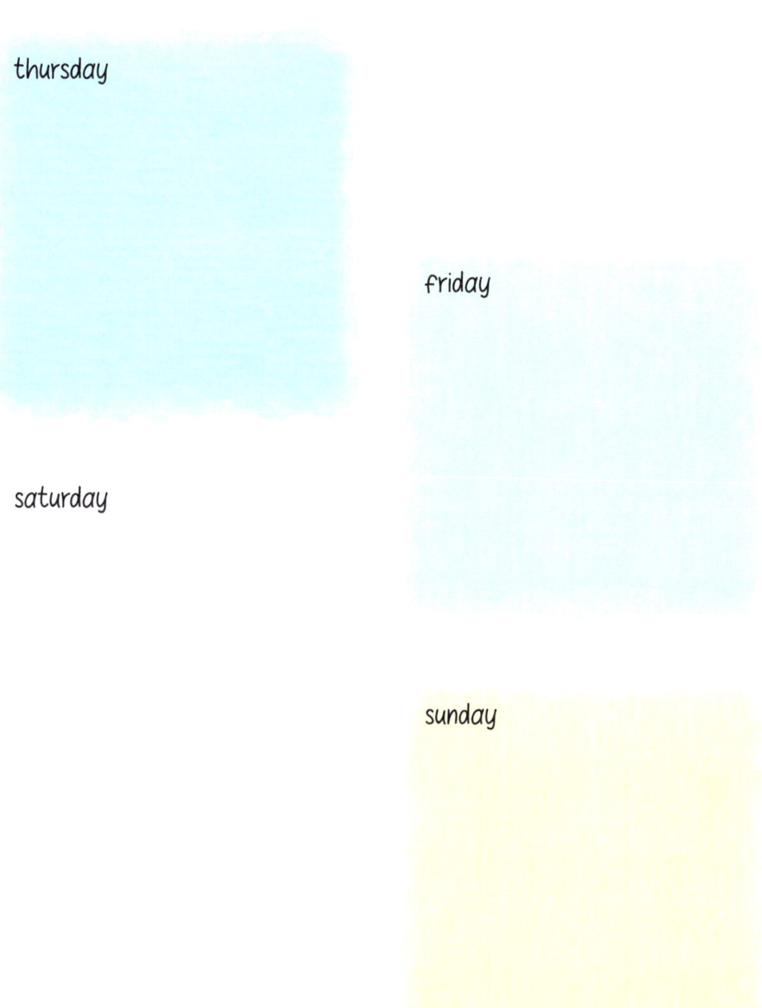

What have you learned about yourself that you can carry forward into the weeks, months, and years to come? What are you ready to let go of so you can live into your best life? Small actions each week will lead to big results.

Well done!

What have you learned about yourself this week? What micro-wins will you celebrate this week? How does it make you feel to acknowledge these achievements?

YOU DID IT!

If you've made it to this page, you have completed a portion of your journey towards living into your best life. Congratulations!!!

How are you going to celebrate?

Yes, it's important that you celebrate.

Even if you simply read the pages of this book without doing the activities, you have taken more action than most people who invest in a book, and the people who buy a book are further ahead than people who take no action at all.

People have positive intentions. They get excited in the moment. They may really want to take action and change how things are in their life. They may want to create a new life for themselves. However, few do what it takes to create the life they say they want.

Why is this? Because people are creatures of habit. Our habits become automatic, and it takes conscious effort to break a habit. To top it off, change can feel uncomfortable, and most people don't want to feel uncomfortable.

You can do it though and there is no reason to wait until things get so painful that you must change or face dire consequences. Face it, when you choose to do something rather than being forced to do it, your results are better, and you make choices that become a way of life.

Thank you for going on this journey with me.

My hope is that you've discovered the value that small, incremental improvements can have on your life. Think back to how things were when you started this book. What has changed? Where would you be if you'd taken no action? What's your next step?

Capture your thoughts on the facing page and keep moving forward on your journey as you Live Into Your Best Life.

Perhaps continuous improvement has become a way of life for you too. Maybe you have become more aware of yourself and others. It's likely that you have increased your emotional intelligence, which will naturally have a ripple effect into all areas of your life.

Continue to live into your best life and focus on how you want your life to be. The rest will come together perfectly.

Enjoy the journey!

Hugs,

Made in the USA
Columbia, SC
06 August 2024

40093118R00122